Early Town Records

of

Rowley, Massachusetts

First Record of the First Church, Copied and Communicated to the Essex Institute

[FROM THE HISTORICAL COLLECTIONS OF THE ESSEX INSTITUTE, VOL. XXXIV, 1898]

GEORGE B. BLODGETTE, ESQ

HERITAGE BOOKS
2008

HERITAGE BOOKS

AN IMPRINT OF HERITAGE BOOKS, INC.

Books, CDs, and more—Worldwide

For our listing of thousands of titles see our website
at
www.HeritageBooks.com

Published 2008 by
HERITAGE BOOKS, INC.
Publishing Division
100 Railroad Ave. #104
Westminster, Maryland 21157

International Standard Book Numbers
Paperbound: 978-0-7884-4898
Clothbound: 978-0-7884-7607-5

EARLY RECORDS OF ROWLEY, MASS.

FIRST RECORD OF THE FIRST CHURCH COPIED AND COMMUNICATED
BY GEORGE B. BLODGETTE, ESQ., OF ROWLEY, MASS.

THE first church in Rowley was gathered December 3, 1639. This record, the first extant, was begun by the Rev. Samuel Shepard, November 15, 1665, the day of his settlement here as colleague with the Rev. Samuel Phillips. There is no evidence known to me of an earlier record in this church.

The following is a list of all the settled ministers of the church :

Ezekiel Rogers,	settled	3 Dec., 1639	died	23 January, 1660–1.
Samuel Phillips	"	June, 1651	"	22 April, 1696.
Samuel Shepard	"	15 Nov., 1665	"	7 April, 1668.
Edward Payson	"	25 Oct., 1682	"	22 Aug., 1732.
Jedidiah Jewett	"	19 Nov., 1729	"	8 May, 1774.
Ebenezer Bradford	"	4 Aug., 1782	"	3 January, 1801.
David Tullar	"	7 Dec., 1803 dismissed 17 Oct., 1810.		

James Tucker	settled	24 June, 1812	dismissed 24 June, 1812.
Willard Holbrook	"	22 July, 1818	" 12 May, 1840.
John Pike	"	18 Nov., 1840	" 5 January, 1869.
Lyman H. Blake	"	9 Nov., 1869	" 27 April, 1874.
William R. Joyslin	"	2 Dec., 1874	" 22 Dec., 1875.
Charles C. Bruce	"	2 July, 1878	" 28 Nov., 1882.

S: Philips his Book

ex dono m^{et} Josiah fflint Aprill 22 1668

Nov : 15, 1665

A Record of Matters in the Church of Rowley from Nov : 15, 1665

Persons in Church estate

Mr Samuel Phillips Teacher soe continued therin since 30 years then octob 25 1682 ordained P. by call of ye ch & advice of y^e [Elders] & Mrs Sarah (his wife) & children Sarah Samuel George Elizabeth Dorcas Mary

Mr Samuel Shepard, p. departed this life Aprill 7 1668

Mr Edward Paifon admitted 15 Octob 1682 ordained Octob : 25 1682 Teacher

Maximillian Jewet Deacon *mortuas*

mort Samuel Broecklebanke Deacon chosen January 8 1665 Ordayned ffebe 18 1665

B^r John Pearfon senior

Deacons ordayned } B^r Ezekiel Jewitt } octob 24 1686 Text 1 Tim. 3. 13
B John Trumble

mort William Tenny Deacon chofen Febe : 3 1667 ordayned June 7 1668

Members in full comunion

Captain Johnfon *mort* | B^r Swan *mortuas*
Mr Nelfon *mort* | Tho : Tenny
B^r Afy | B^r John Harrice

Br Caleb Bointon
Br William Bointon—d—
Mr Nehi Jewett
Br Tho Lambert—d—
Br Wood senior—d—
Br Platts senior
Br Palmer senior
Br Homes
Br Samuel Mighel
Br Prime senior *mort*
Br Langley *mort*
Br Browne—d—
Br foſter
Br James Barker
Br Pearley
Br Joseph Bointon
Br John Pickard Junior
Br Umphrey Hopſon—d—
John Pearſon Junior
John Sawyer

Br Tod
Br Pickard *mortuas*
Mr Tho : Nelſon
Br Barker *mortuas*
Br William Scales *mort*
Br Dreſſer *mort*
Br Pearſon senior
Br John Bayly
Br Birkby
Br leaver senior *mort*
Br Scales John *mort*
Br Leiton *mort*
Br Haſsen *mort*
Barzillo Barker
Br Kilborn *mortuas*
Br Harriman
Br William Jackſon—d—
Br Nicholas Jackſon
Br Trumbl
Br Ezekiel Jewet

Jonathan Wheler
Samuel Broclebank
Samuel Spoffort
Mofes Bradftreet
Able Platts

[torn off]

	Tempus
Barzilla Barker	} March 22 1666
John Watfon	
Ann Jewet Abraham Jewets wife	Aug. 9 1668
Goodwife Trumble	
Goodwife Aufin	Decemb: 8 1668
Goodw: Grant	
Liddeah Borebank	
Ezekiel Jewitt	
John Bayly	
Anthony Aufin	

Women

Ezekiel Jewits wife	March 29 1669
Barzilliai Barkers wife	
Goody Dickefon	
Goody Remington	
Fayth Stickney	
Mary Bointon Laus deo	

Women

Mrs Dumer
Sarah Phillips senior

Goody Simmons Joyned	July 25 1669
Thomas Remmington	
Abraham Hafletine	March 7 1671
Goodw: Browne	
Goodw: Bradftreet	
Goodw: Drefser Johns wife	May 24 1674
Thomas Lamberts wife	Sept. 30 1674
Thomas Lambert	
Thomas Pearly	
Goodw: pearly his wife	ffeb 23 1675
William Fofter	
Goodwife Allye	
John Sawyer his wife } admitted	April 16 1676
Nathaniel Barker his wife	
Caleb Bointon (Williams son) adm	July 2 1676
Mr Neh Jewet & his wife	
Nathaniel Barker	Aprill 18 77
Jofeph Bointon & his wife	
Goodwife Weicom Elizabeth Red-dington	Aug. 12 77

Admitted		At ye sametime Women	
Sarah Kimball of village } admitted	March 31 1677	Mary palmer	May 23 1684
Mary Clark }		Hannah Bointon smiths wife	
Goodw: Coleby		Samuel Dreisers wife	
Goodw: Bointon Johns wife	ffeb 2 1678	Mary Bointon	1684
John peirfon Junior		The 2d wife of Br Sam Plats senior	June 29 1684
John Sawyer		The wife of John Spafford Sarah	Aug 10 1684
John peirfons wife	April 3 1681	The wife of Samuel Spafford Sarah	
Joseph Jewetts wife		Mofes Bradftreet	
John Pickard Junior		Able Platts	
Umphrey Hobfon		Goodwife Homes	June 12 1685
John palmars wife	Septem 6 1682	Mrs Hobfon Junior	
Joseph Chaplins wife		Wife of Br Samuel Platts Junior	
Jachin Reyners wife		Caleb Borebank	
Jonathan Wheler	Novemb 5 1682	Martha his wife	ffeb 21 1685
Hannah [torn off]		Tho: Woods wife	
John Dresser	June 10 1683	Elizabeth Harrice Nath: wife	feb 28 1685
Jofeph Jewitt deacons son		Elizabeth Paifon my daughter	
James Dickinfon		Ruth Jewitt Br Woods daughter	May 30 1686
Samuel Brottlebank	thefe adm:	Mary Peirfon w. Stephen Peifon	July 25 1886
Samuel Spafford	May 23 1684	Colen Frazer	
Samuel Platts		Widdow Scott	June 12 1687
Joseph Chaplin		Hannah Platts	
John Clark		Priscilla Pierson	ffeb 19 1687
Caleb Bointon Smith		Mrs Bennett	May 13 1688
Richard Swan			
James Scales			

Elizabeth [torn off]
ffrances Jewett deacons son
The wife of Caleb Jackfon — January 19 1690
Dorcas[1] Tim : Harries wife — Aprill 27 1690
Benjamin plummers wife
Thomas Ayres wife — June 8 1690
Jonathan Wheelers wife—Baptized — Jully 20 1690
Edward Hafen & his wife Joan — July 26 1691
John Brown, Benjamin Plūmer
Elizabeth Brottlebank, Mercy Dref- fer — Aprill 2 1693
Abigail Brown — April 9 1693
Samuel Bointon & Mary Silver — Octob 15 1693
Hannah Bointon admitted — Octob 8 93
Hannah Bradfreet[2] — Decemb 15 94
Thomas Jewitt
Elizabeth Barker nathaniels daugh- ter — January 14 93
Abigail Stiles
An : ffrazier — Novemb 18 1694
Mr Ezekiel Northen Junior
Mrs Hannah Northen
Mr Thomas Nelfon Junior his wife — Aprill 1695
John Tods wife
Mr Jewts[3] wife
William Creafyes wife

Sarah Coleby mayd
Tho : Spaffords wife — Aprill 1695
Sarah peirfon mayd
Wife of leute John Stickney
Samuel drefers daughter Elizabeth Steward — June 23 1695
Widdow Zear[4]
Elizabeth Bennit
Rebecka Wheeler
Dorithy Coleby   Stew:
Elizabeth Steward James wife — Octob 20 1695
Hannah Ruffell
Ann francis palmers wife — ffeb 9 1695

Persons in full com̄union at the time
men

1 Ed. Paifon
2 Capt Bointon
3 Tho Nelfon
4 Tho Burtble
5 Jno Peirfon
6 Samll Mighel

[1] Tim Harris' wife was Phebe.
[2] This name interlined in original.
[3] Chute.
[4] Searl.

7 Jnº Dreiser
8 Samˡˡ Platts
9 Samˡˡ Brattlebank
10 Jnº Clark
11 Joſ. Chaplin
12 Ezˡˡ. Northend
13 Jonath Wheeler
14 Tim: Harris
15 Samˡˡ Palmer
16 Ed: Hazzen
17 Caleb Bointon
18 Samˡˡ Bointon
19 Samˡˡ Spoford
20 Ben. Pluñer
21 Ezekˡˡ Jewet
22 Joſ Jewet
23 Tho Jewett
24 Jnº Brown
25 Jnº Sawer
26 Nath Barker
27 jer Elſworth
28 Enſign Tenney
29 Jacob Forſter
30 Tho Pearley
31 Neh Jewett
32 Moſ. Bradſtreet
33 Mr Woodman

34 Colin Frazer
35 Benj. Scott
36 Paul Wentworth
37 Aaron Pengry

Perſons admitted to full coñunion ſinc my ordination, numbr from my Day-Book.

1696

84 Eliſabeth Hedden widow } March 29
85 Sarah Nelſon
86 Widow Canady } June 7
87 Abigail Kembal
88 Timothy Harris } July 19
89 Eliſabeth Croſbie
90 Paul Wentworth
91 Catherine Wentworth } Augˢᵗ 30
92 Eſther Burtbe
93 Moſes Bradſtreet
   his wife } feb 28
94 Hannah Bradſtreet

1697

95 Sarah Pickard wife John
   ſometime ſinc diſmiſsed from
   Ipſwich, & admitted here } March 7
96 William Stevens   March 21

97	Benjamin Scott	} June 13
98	Susanna Scott wife Benj.	
99	Mr Josh Woodman	July 25
100	Sarah Laighton	Octobr 17
101	Sarah Nelson wife Phillip	March 6
	ye first Pson admitted in or new-meeting house	

1698

102	Aaron Pengry	} Octobr 30
	& his wife	
103	Ann Pengry	
104	Jane Lambert	Decembr 25
105	Mary Wood, W. Josiah	Janr 22
106	Jeremiah Peirson	
107	Thomas Wood	
108	Josiah Wood	
109	Ebenezer Wood	} ffebruary 5
110	Elisabeth Bayley	
	James Bayleys wife	
111	James Stewart	} ffebruary 12
112	John Stewart	
113	Rachel Wood	

1699

114	Mary Kilborn, w Samll	} March 26
115	Elisabeth Look w. Jonathan	

116	Hannah Broclebank	} Aprill 2
117	Mary Wood	
118	Ann Tenney	
119	David Wheeler senr	} May 7
120	Nathan Wheeler	
121	Samuel Kilborn	
122	Nathanael Brown	
123	Anthony Coleby	} May 14
124	Mary Brown w. Nathanll	} May 21
125	Hannah Jewett w. Thomas	
126	Sarah Jewett w. Maximillian	} June 25
127	Joseph Bointon junr	
	his wife	
128	Bridget Bointon	} July 2
129	Judith Platts wife John	
130	Isaac Jewett	} August 20
	his wife	
131	Dorcas Jewett	

1700

132	Maximillian Jewett	} June 9
133	Andrew Stickney	
134	Elisabeth Stickney	
135	Samuel Ayers	} Octobr 13
136	Abigail Ayers	

1701

137	Jonathan Jewett	
138	Nathan Barker	
139	Mary Jewett w. Jonathan	} Jany 4
140	Sarah Dreiser w. Jonatha.	feb 22

1702

141	Mary Barker Daughter Nathan^ll	May 17
142	Mary Look daughter Jonathan	June 28
143	John Dreiser jun^r	Novemb^r 1

1703

144	Tho. Burtbe	
145	Ezek^ll Laighton	
146	Mrs Woodman	} Jun 20
147	Rebekka Laighton	
148	Dunkin Stewart	Septr 26
149	Phebe Coleman	feb. 13

1704

150	Jonathan Jackfon	
	his wife	} July 2
151	Hannah Jackfon	
152	Abigail Clark wife Rich^d	
153	Hefter Barker	

154	Jacob Barker	
	his wife	} Aug^st 20
155	Margaret Barker	
156	Sarah Jewet wife	
	of Abraham	
157	Mofes Platts	Octob^r 1
158	Damaris Leaver widow	} ffeb^y 4
159	Elifabeth Tenney	

1705

160	Hannah Clark w. Judah	} March 25
161	Mary Jackfon D. Caleb	
162	Jofeph Scott	
163	Jofeph Jewett	
164	Margaret Chaplin	} May 20
	w. John	
165	Sarah Hopkinfon	
	w. Michael	
166	Hannah Lancafter	
167	Dorcas Hobfon	} May 27
168	Jane Peirfon	
169	Samuel Dreiser	
	his wife	} July 15
170	Mary Dreiser	
171	Sarah Bayley	
172	Elifabeth Jackfon	

173	Sarah Scales	Sept 2
174	Martha Pelfron D. Stephen	d m
175	Mary Duty D. William	2 — 10
1706		
176	Judah Trumble	March 3
177	Sister Greenough	
178	Daniel Jewett & his wife	July 28
179	Elifabeth Jewett	
1707		
180	Abraham Coleby	July 13
181	Enfign Andrew Stickney	ffebr 8
182	Mary Jewet w. Joseph	
1708		
183	Br Robt. Greenough senr.	May 9
184	Elifabeth Platts wife Isaac	Augst 8
185	Lydia Jackfon D. Jonathan	
186	Phebe Harris Dr. Deacon Harris	
1709		
187	Nathll Jewett	Septr 4
188	Lydia White	
189	Mary Jewett w. Nathll	Octobr 23
1710		
190	Huldah Bridges w. Jno	Novr 26
191	Elifabeth Jewett	December 31

1711		
192	Ephraim Nelfon	Sept 2
193	& Sarah Nelfon	
194	Ruth Bointon Maid	ffebr 24
1712		
195	Martha Smith w. Benjam.	May 18
1713		
196	Thomas Lambert	Sept 13
197	William Geage	
198	Jeremiah Chaplin	
199	Sarah Lambert	
200	Ann Chaplin	
201	Prifcila Jewet	
1714		
202	James Platts	April 18
	his wife	
203	Lydia Platts	
204	Aquilla Jewett	April 25
205	Mercy Geage	
206	Abigail Hodgkin	Jun 13
207	Mary Payfon	
208	Dorothy Rogers	Augst 1
209	Elifabeth Heyden	
210	Sarah Prime w. Samll	Sept 12
211	Anne Prime	

212	Sarah Palmer	Octobr 31
	Anne Bointon	
213	Stephen Jewett	ffebr 28
214	Priscilla Jewett	
215	Deborah Searls	1715
216	Hagar my Indian Maid	Augst 14
217	Mary Elithorp wife Jno	Septr 25
		1716
218	Mary Sawer wife Jno	Septr 9
219	Nathll Bayly	Janry 27
		1717
220	Willim Hobson	March 17
221	Sarah Hobson	
222	Benjamin Smith	Jun 2
223	Priscilla Bointon	Augst 4
224	Saml Woodberry	Sept. 15
225	Ellsabeth Hopkinson w. Jer.	
226	Jno Hartshorn	Febr 23
227	Rebecca Burtby	
		1718
228	Robert Choate	April 6
229	Samuel Nelson	
230	Eunuce Choate	
231	Joseph Bayley	April 13
232	Sarah Scott w. Benj.	
233	Jeremiah Elsworth	Jun 3
234	Hannah Elsworth	
235	Martha Dickinson	
236	Ruth Tenny	July 20
237	Sarah Harris	
238	John Bointon	Augst 31
	his wife	
239	Bithiah Bointon	
240	Bridget Hamon	
		1719
241	Esf. Jno Hobson	March 29
242	Hilkiah Bointon	
243	Moses Davis	
	his wife	
244	Hannah Davis	May 10
245	Johannah Dreiser	
246	Johannah Pickard	Septr 20
247	James Barker	
		1720
248	Jane Clark wife Jonath.	May 1
249	Edna Pickard	Septr 18
		1721
250	Francis Pickard	Sept 17
251	Ann Stewart widow	
	thot to be nearer a 100 yn 90 years	
252	Damaris Dickinson	

253	Martha Nevins a Scotch Woman	Septr 24
254	Jeremiah Burtby	Octobr 29
255	Mary Peirſon	Novembr 5
256	Mary Killborn	Decembr 10
257	Dorcas Killborn	
258	Humphery Hobſon	Febry 11
259	Mehetable Hobſon	
260	Sarah Scott	

1722

An awfull dead year! not one admitted.

1723

261	Priſcilla Jewett	Aprill 28
262	Stephen Peirſon & his wife	
263	Hannah Peirſon	Augt 4
264	Suſannah Todd	
265	Eliſabeth Davis	
266	Amos Pilſberry & his	
267	wife Eliſabeth	
268	John Northend	Septr 22
269	Lydia Rogers	
270	Cornelious Davis	
271	John Jewett	
272	Mary Killborn widow	Novemr 10
273	Miriam Jackman widow	

274	Job Pengry	Decembr 29
	his wife	
275	Elizabeth Pengry	
276	Abigail Kelly	
277	Capt. Samll. Pickard	Febry 16
	his wife	
278	Eliſabeth Pickard	
279	Eliſabeth Payſon	

1724

280	Mary Davis wife Jno.	April 12
281	Patience Palmr wife Timothy	Feb. 21

1725

282	Jemima Bennet	April 21
283	Mary Trumble	July 11

1726

284	Joshua Jackſon	May 22
285	Danll Foster &	Jun 26
286	his wife Hannah	

1727

287	George Hybirt & wife	Augt 13
288	Sarah Hybirt	
289	John Bayley	
	his wife	
290	Eliſabeth bayley	Octobr 1
291	Jonathan Birtby	

292	Edward Payfon	
293	James Platts	
	& his wife	
294	Mercy Platts	
295	John Johnfon	Decembr 3
296	Daniel Johnfon	
	his wife	
297	Hannah Johnfon	
298	Eliphalet Payfon	December 10
299	Samuel Payfon	
300	Edna Payfon	
301	Mary Payfon	
302	Mary Stewart	Decembr 17
303	Dorthy Northen	
304	John Todd junr	
305	his wife Ruth Todd	Decembr 21
306	Lydia Bishop	
307	Samuel Scott	
308	Ebenefar Burtby	
309	Anna Lull	
310	Rebecar Deuty	Decembr 24
311	Miriam Birtby	
312	Elifabeth Scott	
313	Martha Creafie	
314	Capt. Thomas Hale & his wife	
315	Edna Hale	Decembr 31
316	Sarah Bifhop	Janry 7
317	Bridgett Bointon	
318	Sarah Todd	Janry 14
319	Mehetabel Jewet	
320	Hannah Birtby	
321	John Harris	Janry 21
322	Daniel Ritter	
323	Lydia Ritter	
324	Nathan Frazer	
325	Sarah Platts	Janry 28
326	Elifabeth Harris	
327	Elifabeth Plummer	
328	Sarah Bayly	
329	Mary Jewet wife Jofhua	Febry 25
330	Sarah Jewet Dr Nathanll.	
331	James Todd	
332	Thomas Wood	Febry 4
333	Samll Duty	
334	Mary Todd	
335	Elifabeth Payfon my wife	ffeb. 18
	1728	
336	Samuel Killborn	
337	Samuel Heyden	March 10
338	Hannah Woodberry	
339	Dorothy Bointon	
340	Mercy Scott	Aprill 21

341	Daniel Drefser	Aprill 28
342	Elifabeth Killborn	
343	Faith Platts	Jun 9
344	Jonathan Pickard	
345	Aaron Pengry	October 20
346	Mercy Clark	
347	Mehetabel Northen	February 2
	Jedidiah 1729 Jewett	
348	Elifabeth Payfon wife David	July 8
349	Jane Jewet Dr Nathanll	Augst 24
350	Lydia Pickard wife Mofes	
351	Elifabeth Jewet Dr Aquilla	Octobr. 19
	Hannah Crefey wife of Abel per me	
	1730	
352	Jofeph Dr Todd	
353	Richard Esty	Aprill 19
	his wife	
354	Ruth Esty	
355	Enoch Dole &	Novembr 22
	his wife	
356	Rachel Dole	
357	George Jewet and	february 7th
	his wife	
358	Hannah Jewet	
359	Thomas Lancaster	
360	Mehetabell Jewet	

	1731	
	Samuel Drefser Junr	March 4
361	Sarah Tenny wife Samll	April 25
362	Jane Hobfon w. Jeremiah	Septr 5
363	Hannah Sawyer	Dec. 19
	Jane Frazer wife of Nathan	Jan. 30
	1732	
364	Mrs Jewet w. of or Mr Jewet	March 26
	Since my coming till now 22 taken in	
22	Jonathan Chaplin &	Aug. 6
23	His wife Sarah	
24	Nathan Woodberry	
	1733	
25	Mary Drefser	March 4
26	Samuel Kelly	June 6
27	Lydia Hobfon wife of Mofes	Aug. 26
	1734	
28	Thomas Ritter	March 10
29	Jofhua Prime	
	1735	
30	Hannah Bradftreet wife of Nathll.	Sep. 7
31	Ruth Jewet wife of Eliphalet	Sep. 14
32	David Jewet student	Oct. 12
33	Hannah Woodberry	Nov. 2
34	Eliphalet Jewet	Jan. 4

1736

35	Mercy Bayley	Feb. 8
36	David Bayley	
37	Mercy Sawyer	June 20
38	Bethiah Jewet	
39	John Pearſon	July 4
40	Mary Bayley w. of David	Aug. 8
41	Eben Hidden	Oct. 31
42	Elisabeth Jewet wife of Jacob	Nov. 28
43	Sarah Gage	

1737

44	Mary Woodberry datr. of Samll	Feb. 27
45	Mary Pingry da.tr of Aaron	April 24
46	Elizabeth Palmer w. of Daniel	
47	Joseph Burpee	May 29
48	Elizabeth Prime wife of Doctr	July 24

1738

49	Mark Jewet	
50	Mary Jewet his wife	Dec. 17
51	Hannah Palmer	

1739

52	Daniel Palmer	Jan. 14
53	Martha Scot	
54	Hannah Boynton	Jan. 21
55	Ezekiel Sawyer	
56	Sarah Elsworth	Feb. 11

57	Priſcilla Mighil	March 11
58	Bethiah Boynton	
59	Mary Palmer datr. of John	March 18
60	Capt. Nathanael Mighil	March 25
61	Joanna Kilborn	Nov. 4
62	Mary Hammond	

1740

63	Michael Creſey in his 80th year	May 4
64	William Duty	
65	Sarah Cresey wife of John	Aug. 24

1741

66	Priſcilla Mighil Junr	March 22
67	Jane Osborn wife John	April 5
68	Mary Jewet datr of Joſeph	
69	Mary Jewet wife of Jeremy	May 3
70	Hannah Mighil	
71	Margaret Wood wife of Thomas	May 10
72	Moſes Kefar	May 17
73	Hannah Scot	May 31
74	James Hidden	June 21
75	Jeremiah Todd	July 19
76	Jonathan Smith	
77	Eliſabeth Payſon	
78	Aaron Clark	Aug. 9
79	Hannah Elsworth	

80	Elisabeth Lowel	⎱ March 7
81	Hannah Barker	⎰
82	Elisabeth Ritter	Feb. 28
83	Mercy Smith	March 21
84	Rebekah Lowel	⎫
85	Sarah Northend	⎪
86	Nathanael Jewet jun^r.	⎬ April 4
87	Caleb Jewet	⎪
88	Mehetabel Hidden	⎪
89	Mehetabel Chaplin	⎭
90	Sarah Payson	April 11
91	Nathanael Bradstreet	⎱ April 18
92	and Hannah his wife	⎰
93	Elisabeth Smith	⎱ May 23
94	Mehetabel Roufe	⎰
95	Isaac Burpee	May 30
96	Susanna Hibbert	Oct. 17
97	Ezekiel Northend	⎱ Nov. 21
98	John Crosby	⎰
99	Jeremy Jewet son of Aquila	Jan 2
100	Jeremy Burpee	
101	Hannah Evans	
102	Jane Sanders 1742	⎱ March 7
103	Nathan Plats his wife	
104	Elisabeth Plats	

105	Lucy Hidden	⎱ Aug. 16
106	Susanna Scot	⎰
107	Mary Dreiser wife of Daniel	
108	Mary Brown	⎱ Aug. 30
109	Benjamin Smith jun^r	⎰
110	John Jewet	Oct. 11
111	Moses Davis jun^r	
112	Elisabeth Hodgskins	⎱ Oct. 18
113	Elisabeth Pickard	⎰
114	Sarah Crosbey	
115	Dinah Mr Northends Negroe girl	⎱ Nov. 1
116	James Jewet	⎰
117	Elisabeth Boynton	Nov. 8
118	Ephraim Boynton	Nov. 29
119	Ann Jewet	⎱ Jan. 3
120	Stephen Palmer son of Francis	⎰
121	Stephen Palmer son of Timothy	⎱ Feb. 14
122	Jonathan Clark	⎰
123	Thomas Mighill	
124	John Tenny	Feb. 21
	Nathanael Mighill jun^r	
	1743	
125	Thomas Gage & Apphia his wife	⎱ March 7
126	John Chaplin jun^r	⎰
127	Mary Barker wife of Jacob	

128	Abigail Atwood w. of Anthony	Sep. 9
129	Mary Pearson	Nov. 27
	1744	
130	Jonathan Tredwell	July 15
131	Priscilla Foster wife of Abraham	Oct. 21
132	Hannah Day	Nov. 18
133	Stephen Jewet junr.	Feb. 17
	About 208 persons at present in full Communion with this Chh. 83 males 125 Females.	
134	Bethiah Bradford	March 30
135	Abigail Kilborn w. of Ebenezer	Nov. 3
136	Amos Jewet }	
137	Ruth Pierson wife of John }	Feb. 9
	1746	
138	Ruth Tredwell w. of Jonathan	July 27
139	Mary Hibbert	Aug. 31
140	Priscilla Hobson	Jan. 11
141	Ruth Mr Bradstreets negroe woman	Jan. 11
142	Sarah Pickard w. of Capt. Saml.	Jan. 18
	1747	
143	Jane Bayley wife of Saml.	Oct. 18
	1748	
144	Thomas Tenny and }	
145	his wife }	July 10
	1749	
	1750 awful dead years.	
	1751 none taken into full Comm.	
	1752	
146	Sarah Davis	May 31 1752
	The first person admitted in our new meeting house	
147	Anna Elsworth w. of Jeremy junr.	Aug. 16
	1753	
148	Martha Jewet wife of Thomas	Apr. 1
149	Mary Jewet wife of Aquila	July 8
	· 1754	
150	Priscilla Jewet datr. of Aquila	Feb.
151	Elisabeth Mighll	Dec. 1 1754
	1755	
152	Sarah Pearson wife of Jonathan	Dec. 7
153	Lucy Bradstreet wife of Moses	Dec. 14
	1756	
154	Sarah Coopar wife of Leonard }	
155	Elisabeth Smith wife of Benjamin }	Feb. 1
156	Jemima Scot w. of Joseph }	
157	David Pickard & }	
158	Abigail his wife }	March 14
159	Joseph Scott	March 21
160	Ednah Todd	June 6

1757

| 161 | Hannah Johnson wife of Jonathan | May 15 |
| 162 | Widow Sarah Pearson | Aug. 14 |

1758

1759

| 163 | Mary Elsworth w. of Nathanael | Feb. 18 |

1760

| 164 | Mehetabel Bailey w. of David | Feb. 24 |

1761

| 165 | Jacob Low | } March 15 |
| 166 | Sarah his wife | |

1762

167	Hannah Wood w. of Jonathan	May 31
168	Mary Payson datr. of Saml	June 7
169	Samuel Bayley	July 26

1764

170	Sarah Brocklebank	April 15
171	Jonathan Pearson	May 6
172	David Searl	May 20
173	Ann Brocklebank wife of Nathan	
174	Hannah Pearson dtr. of Jonathan	} May 27
175	Elisabeth Brocklebank dtr Nathan	
176	Eunice Hidden wife of Price	June 3
177	Rebekah Palmer wife of Francis junr.	} June 10

178	Bridget Prime wife of Joshua	
179	John Bayley junr	
180	Ezekiel Bayley	} July 15
181	Nathan Pearson	
182	Hannah Elsworth	
183	Abigail Todd w. of John	
184	Mary Palmer w. of Stephen	
185	Anne Todd w. of James	} Aug. 26
186	Hannah Hobson dtr. of Moses	
187	Abel Creisy junr.	
188	Stephen Jewett junr.	
189	Sarah Creisy wife of James	Sep. 23
190	Widow Mary Cooper	Sep. 30
191	Moses Bradstreet	
192	Elisabeth Creisy wife of Mark	Oct. 14
193	Anne Hobson	
193	Phebe Bradstreet w. of Nathll.	Nov. 18
194	Eunice Duty	
195	Jeremiah Pickard	
196	John Bradstreet	Dec. 9

1765

197	Humphry Sanders & his wife	Jan. 13
198	Jane Sanders	
199	Joseph Pickard	Feb. 17
200	Elisabeth Stickney w. of David	Mar. 10

201	Moses Clark	March 31
202	Sarah Pearson	April 21
203	Mary Dreser w. of David	June 16
204	Elizabeth Dickinson w. of Thomas	Oct. 27
205	Hannah Platts wife of Mark	Dec. 29

1766.

206	Elisabeth Jewett w. of Stephen junr.	June 8
207	Lydia Sanders dr. of Edward	
208	Elizabeth Todd w. of Asa	June 29
209	Lydia Hobson w. of William	
210	William Jewett	Sep. 7

1767

211	Priscilla Perkins	April 12
212	Eunice Harris w. John junr.	
213	Judith Searl w. of David	June 28
214	Eunice Dickinson w. of Moses	Aug. 16
215	Widow Susanna Stickney	Aug. 23

1768

| 216 | Jane Jewett w. of Deacon Jeremiah | Jan. 28 |

1769, 70, 71, 72 awfully dead years

1773

217	Mr Thomas Lancaster junr	Oct. 3
218	& Lydia his wife	
219	Sarah Pickard wife of Joshua	Oct. 31

HIST. COLL. VOL. XXXIV

1774

Thomas Mighill Recorder

1775

| 1 | Sarah Stickney wife of Moses | April 30th 1775 |

1776

| 2 | Mary Marten the Daugr. of Nathanal | Feb. 15 1776 |

1777

3	Bethiah Dreser Dr. Samuel	
4	Hannah Chaplin Dr. Dean. Chaplin	April 13th 1777
5	Martha How Dr. Philimon	
6	Hannah Pearly wife John	July 19th 1778
7	Ruth Boynton wid. woman	Nov. 8th 1778
8	Elizabeth Jewett wife of David	January 10th 1779
9	Rachel Mighill wife Thomas	July 10th 1780
10	Elisabeth Jewett Dat. of Dean.	January 28th 1781
11	Jane Pickard wife John	April the 29th 1781
12	Mehetabel Hidden	June 10th 1781

The Revd. Ebenezer Bradford came to Rowley to take the charge of the Chh.   May 31st 1782

Owned ye Covent
1690 July 29

A list of the persons that desired upon ye foresayed day to own the covenant

Tho: Dickinson
John Dickinson
Mercy Dickinson
Jonathan Nelson
Gershom Nelson
Hannah Nelson
William Bointon
Jeremiah Hopkinson
Michael Hopkinson
Ester Hopkinson
Tho: Jewitt
Ezekiel Jewitt
Maxemillian Jewitt
William Jewitt

Joseph Thurston owned ye covent — febry 5, 1698-9
John Nelson — May 7 1699
Samll Hedden — March 5 1699

1700

Judah Trumble
his wife Elisabeth
John Hobson
his wife Dorcas
Joseph Peirson } March 3

James Tod
Jonathan Dresser } March 17
Samll Dresser
Sarah Dresser } March 31
Thomas Geage
Mary Geage } July 14
Thomas Lambert
& his wife
Sarah Lambert
Mary Tod wife James
Mary Nelson wife Jno.
Jonathan Woodman
& his wife Sarah
Margaret Bointon D. Caleb
Mary Barker Dr. Nathanaell } January 19

1701

Danll Jewett
& his wife Elisabeth
Hannah Kilborn } Augst. 3
Elisabeth Jackson
Mary Jackson
Nathanll Elithorp
Benjamin Stickney
Nathanll Bayley } Sept. 21

1702

Mary Stickney wife of Benjamin	Sept. 21
Sarah Bayley wife Nathanael	
Ann Kilborn	
Margaret Tenney	Octobr. 19
Johanna Barker	
Ruth Bointon	
Elifabeth Kilborn	
Richard Bointon	
Jno. Bointon	Decembr 28
Jno. Chaplin	
ffrancis Nelfon	
Jacob Barker	

Ebenezr. Hedden	August 2
Joseph Jewett	
Jno. Decker	
Ellfab Greenough	
Jeremiah Nelfon & his wife	Augst 23
Ann Nelfon	
Goody Hedden wife Eben	

1703

Aquila Jewett	July 11
Ann Pengry	July 24

Hester Barker	Nov. 21
James Dickinfon	decem. 19
Lionel Cheute	

1704

Jno. Drefer & his wife Margaret	March 5
Judah Clark	
Robt. Rogers	
Sarah Jewett	March 26
wife Abraham	
Mark Prime	
Henry Pore junr.	June 5
Jofeph Scott	
Mary Drefser w. Samll. junr.	July 16
Anne Mighell	July 23
Nicholas Wallingford	Augst. 27
William Creafie	
John Plumer & wife	Novr. 5
Abigail Plumer	
Elizabeth Tenney D. Tho:	
Jofhua Woodman	
Mehetabel his wife	
Mary Laighton	
Mary Duty	

1705

Isaac Platts & his wife Elifabeth	
Samuel Dickinfon & his wife Ruth	April 8
Jeremiah Chaplin	
Benoni Bointon	
Sarah Prime	
Anne Prime	
Sarah Scott	
Sarah Scales	June 24
Elifabeth Decker	
Elifabeth Peirfon	
Martha Peirson	July 15
Bithia Platts	
Sarah Harris	Augst. 27
Ezekiel Sawer & his wife	
Hannah Sawer	Septr 9
George Dickinfon & his wife	
Martha Dickinfon	Decembr. 2
Robert Greenough his wife	
Hannah Greenough	
Dorothy Rogers	ffebry. 3

1706

John Scott	
Joh Davis & his wife Davis	ffebry. 17
Nathanll. Mighel his wife	
Prifcilla Mighell	
Samll. Brattlebank his wife	
Sarah Brattlebank	
Phebe Harris	Octobr. 13.

1707

Tho Tenney his wife	
Sarah Tenney	March 23
Jofeph Drefser	
Jeremiah Hopkinfon	
Robert Day & his wife	
Elifabeth	May 11
Jofeph Nelfon	Jun 29
Samll. Prime and his wife	
Sarah Prime	Nov. 9
Mary Jewett w. Jofeph	Nov. 16
Nathanll. Jewet & his wife	Nov. 23.

1708

Georg Hybert
Prifcilla Jewet wife Nehem̄ } Novr. 30

Mary Payfon
Mehetabel Payfon
Lydia Jackfon } May 9
Nehemiah Jewet
Prifcilla Jewet } June 6
Hannah Sawer
Mary Jackfon } Augst. 8
William Bennet
Saml. Palmer } Decembr. 5

1709

Benjamin Smith & his wife Martha
William Geage &'s wife Mercy } July 17
Stephen Jewett
Aron Pengry } Octobr. 2
Hagar Indus } October 9
Hilkiah Boynton } Novr. 27
John Searl & his wife Elifabeth
Jonathan Jewett & his wife Anne
Prifcilla Bointon w. Hilkiah } Jany. 15
Noah Barker

1710

Jofeph Kilborn & his wife Mary } July 9
John Smith } Septembr 17

Ephraim Nelfon & his wife Sarah
Sarah Highbirt w. George } Novr. 19
Jno. Bridges & Amos Pilsberry
Jonathan Pickard & his wife & Sarah Scot 31-10 } Decembr. 3

1711

Jno. Palmer & his wife Mary } June 17

1712

Stephen Peirfon & his wife
Humphery Hobfon
Eliphelet Payfon } March 9
Samuel Payfon
Jno Sawyer } July 27
Tho Palmer & his wife Sarah
Thomas Wood Simons's } Novr. 9
Henry & Abigail Elithorp
Tho Wood & his wife Sarah } Decembr. 7
George Kilborn & his wife Phebe } Jany 4

1713

Mofes Davis & his wife Hannah } May 17
Edna Northend & Johanna Geage } Jun 25

1714

Jeremiah Elfworth & his wife Hannah
Samuel Tenny & his wife Ann } Jun 6
Jemima Bennet & Hannah Nelfon } Jun 13

Edward Payfon
Nathanˡˡ. Hamõn
Bridget Hammon   } Augˢᵗ 29
Debrah Searls
Elifabeth White
Ebenezer Clark
Elifabeth Donnel   } Octobʳ. 17
Damaris Leaver

1715

Francis Pickard
Jnº Bennet
Mary Bennet   } May 11
Lydia Clark
William Duty & his wife   } Augˢᵗ. 14
Jofhua Jewett & his wife } Janʳʸ. 3

1716

Benj. Scott & his wife
Jeremiah Burtby & his wife } March 24
Samˡˡ Stickney & his wife   } Septʳ. 2
Danˡˡ. Thurfton &'s wife   } Novʳ. 25
Jnº Tod & his wife   } ffeb. 3

1717

Isaac Kilborn & his wife Dorcas
Jofeph Bayley
Sarah Barker w. James   } Jun 23
Ruth Tenney

Edw. Saundrs. & Elifabeth his wife   } July 27
Elleonar Bolnton   } Septʳ. 1
Tho Nelfon & his wife   } Octobʳ. 13
Richard Dole & his wife   } Novʳ. 17
Sarah Wood wife Tho.
Samˡˡ Scott & his wife Betty
Francis Palmr. & his wife Sarah   } Feb. 23
Elifabeth Payson
Hannah Payfon

1718

Jane Northend   } May 18
Sarah Duty
Jonath Clark & his wife
Job Pengry & his wife   } Octobʳ. 26
Mofes Pickard & his wife
Dorothy Nelfon
Jonathan Creafie   } ffeb. 1
Nathˡˡ. Crosbie

1719

Samuel Deuty   } July 5
Lydia Todd
Tho Birtby
  & his wife   } Octobʳ. 4
Mary Birtby

1720

James Jarvis & his wife   } Aprill 10
  Mary

David Hammon and his wife Mary
Mary Platts } Jun 5

Sarah Palmer
Ann Palmer
Mary Stewart
Elifabeth Crosbie
Hephziba Pierfon
Mehetabel Tenny } Octobr. 23

Sarah Pierson wife Joseph } Janry. 15

Mary Pierson
Martha Dreifer } Janry. 29

1721

John Northend
Eliot Payfon
James Platts & his wife
Hannah Platts
Sufanna Scott
Mary Trumble
Dorothy Northend } Sept. 17

Mary Lambert } Octr. 22.
Abigail Rows } Octr. 29.
Jonathan Shepard
Jnᵒ. Creaie & his wife } January 28

1722

James Brown & his wife Mary } March 1
Mofes Bradftreet & his wife Abigail } July 1

Samuel Kilborn
Ebenezer Birtby & his wife Miriam } Augˢᵗ. 15

Aaron Plumer his wife Elifabeth } Decembr. 16

1723

Mary Birtby
Sufannah Todd
Elifabeth Davis
Abigail Clark
Jonathan Birtby & his wife Hañah } March 10

Timothy Palmer & his wife Patienc
John Dickinfon & his wife Sufanna
John Bayley } Septʳ. 22.

Samˡ. Jewett & his wife Jemima } Decemʳ. 15

Mary Payfon Eliot
Payfons wife } Feb. 2.

1724

Tho Dickinfon
& his wife
Elifab. Dickinfon
John Dreiser junr — April 5
— Febry. 7

1725

Jedidiah Kilborn
Daniel Foster &
his wife Hannah
Mary Bradftreet w. Mofes junr.
Hannah Northen
Mehetabel Northen
Sarah Lambert
Edna Prime
Jeremiah Dow and
his wife
Bridget Bointon — June 6
Mary Mighell
Sarah Plummer
Elifabeth Harris
Hannah Harris — Augst [date worn off]
Ezekll. Northen
James Bayly
Abel Platts
& his wife
Mary Platts — Febry. 6

John Stickney
& his wife
Ann Stickney
Jofhua Jackfon
Jane Dreiser — Febry. 6

1726

John Harris
Elifabeth Palmer — March 6
David Kilborn
& his wife &
Eliph Kilborns wife — Aprll. 24
Sarah Bayly
wife of Jofeph
Daniel Johnfon — May 15
& his wife hanah
John Jonfon — Sept 18
Mofes Hobfon
& his wife Lydia
Benjamin Jewet
& his wife Dorothy — Novbr. 13

1727

Samuel Creafie
& his wife Mary
Nathanll Bradftreet
Jane Bradftreet
Mehetabel Jewett — Novembr. 5

Novembr 26

December 10

Joseph Creasie
Samuel Dreiser junr
Hannah Birtby
Ann Jewett
Jeremiah Todd
Thomas Prime
Nathan Jewett
Joseph Pickard
Mary Pickard
Jane Pickard
Daniel Todd
Samuel Heyden
David Bayley
John Peirson
David Birtby
Nathan Birtby
Richard Peirson
Jonathan Todd
Ezekiel Sawyer
Samuel Birtby
Ephrim Bointon
Zacheus Bointon
Ezra Jewett
John Jewett

Novembr 5

Novembr. 26

Elizabeth Northen
Dorothy Bointon
Mary Bointon
Mercy Scott
Hephzibah Platts
Sarah Jewet
Mehetabel Jewett
Phebe Jewett
Eliphelet Killborn
Thomas Lancaster
Ann Bayley
Mary Johnson
Jane Prime
Hannah Lambert
Edna Lambert
Abigail Hodgkin
Mary Hodgkin
Sarah Platts
Martha Creasie
Sarah Price
Mary Leaver
Hannah Lancaster
Mary Heyden
David Payson
Nathan Phrazer
Daniel Dreiser
George Jewett

Dan^ll Palmer
Hannah Bayly
Elifabeth Bifhop
Sarah Geage
Jane Jewett
Mercy Clark
Hannah Hopkinfon
Thomas Geage
Hannah Scott
Mehetabel Scott
David Pearley
Samuel Platts
Sarah Platts
Samuel Northen
Samuel Prime
Jacob Jewet
Mehetable Todd
Sufannah Paifon
Elifabeth Chaplin
David Jewett
Jofeph Scott
Mark Prime
Mofes Smith
Mercy Bayley
Samuel Bayly
Rachel Jewett
Hannah Sawyer
} December 17

} Decemb^r. 24

Edna Bointon
Elifabeth Jewett
Jofeph Duty
Thomas Wood jun^r.
Lucy Tuttle
Sarah Stewart
Anne Stickny
David Jewett
Eliphalet Jewet
Elifabeth Jewett
Martha Hobfon
Mary Spofford
Sam^ll. Woodberry jun^r.
Mercy Barker
Jacob Barker
Bithiah Bointon
Aaron Drefser
Ruth Pickard
Hannah Bifhop
David Creafie
Samuel Bayly
Mercy Jewett
Elifabeth Lull
Mehetabel Chaplin
Hannah Bointon
Hannah Todd
Mary Drefser
} Decemb^r. 24

} Jan^ry. 21

} Jan^ry 28

Hannahr Hammon
Abigail How
Patience Pearly
Jonathan Johnfon
Hannah Scott
Mary Hopkinfon

1728

Jan⸴ 28

Elifabeth Tenny
Abigail Jewett
Sarah Elfworth
Elifabeth Smith
Mercy Smith
Hannah Dreifer
Abigail Jackfon
Abell Creafle
Hannah Creafle
Elifabeth Appleton now Payfon
Mehetabell Dreifer
Mary Davis
Faith Platts
Rebecka Dreifer

March 31

Mercy Sawyer
Mary Woodberry
Mary Birtby
Mehetabell Killborn
Elifabeth Hopkinson

Septemr. 1.

Hanna Barker
Edward Chapman
  his wife
Ruth Chapman
Look for yᵉ next in pag 110

Septemr. 1.

Those who have owned the Covenant since my settlement here

1728

1 Richard Eastick — Jan. 26

1729

2 Elisabeth Palmer & — July 8
3 Rebekah Pingry
4 Mercy Sawyer — July 13
5 Mary Woodberry — Feb. 8
6 Jeremiah Hobfon

1730

7 Leonard Cooper — March 15
8 Hannah Todd w. Jonathan — March 8
9 Abigail Clark — Oct. 4
10 Mofes Cooper

1731

11 Abraham Jewet — Aug. 29
12 Jonathan Nelfon
13 Jofeph Hedden
14 Mark Jewet

1732
15 Sarah Mighil

1733
16 Bethiah Jewet

17 Eben Hidden
18 & his wife Mehetabel   Feb. 18
19 Rebekah Metcalf   Apr. 22
20 Sarah Barker   May 6
21 James Hibbert   June 3
22 Daniel Martin &
23 His wife Rebekah   July 8
24 Thomas Lambert junr.
25 His wife Elizabeth   Aug. 12

1734
26 Thomas Ritter   Jan. 27
27 Hannah Woodberry   Apr. 7
28 Mofes Kafar   June 30
29 George Dickinfon
30 & His wife ——   Sep. 15
31 James Baker junr.
32 & his wife ——   Jan. 12
33 Richard Lowel   Feb. 9

1735
34 Sarah Thurston
35 Mary Hammond   March 16
36 Phebe Harris
37 Margaret Chaplin   June 1

1736
38 Mofes Jewet
39 William Bennet   March 7
40 Elisabeth Gage   Apr. 11
41 Eliſabeth Scot   May 9
42 Martha Scot
43 Jonathan Pickard
44 Joseph Burpee
45 Elisabeth Sanders   May 30
46 Ann Palmer
47 Elisabeth Ritter
48 Hannah Mighil
49 Ruth Todd
50 Thomas Barker
51 Benjamin Smith junr.
52 Humphry Hobfon junr.
53 Abel Jewet
54 James Jewet
55 Nathanael Barker
56 Mary Pingry
57 Joanna Kilborn   June 13
58 Mary Palmer
59 Priſcilla Mighil
60 Mary Clark
61 Lucey Hedden

62 Joſhua Woodman
63 Nathan Plats } July 18
64 Nathan Lambert
65 Jonathan Smith
66 Affa Nelſon
67 Eliſabeth Clark } July 18
68 Sarah Northend
69 Mary Kilborn
70 Rebekah Lowel
71 Hannah Palmer
72 Bethiah Biſhop
73 Sarah Stickney } July 25
74 Sarah Jewet
75 Mary Jewet
76 Jane Lambert } Aug 8
77 Joanna Pickard
78 Mary Candage } Aug. 22
79 Hannah Kilborn
80 Sarah Payſon
81 Sarah Chapman wife of Edward } Sep. 5
82 Mehetabel Prime w. of Joſhua } Sep. 19
83 Mary Kaſar
84 Moſes Hopkinſon } Nov. 7.
85 & Mary his wife
86 Mary Jewet wife of Mark } Nov. 7.
87 Suſanna Scot

88 Elisabeth Payſon daᵗʳ. of Eliot } Dec. 5.
89 Hannah Syles } Dec. 19
90 Hannah Elsworth

1737

91 Nathanael Mighil junʳ. July 24
92 Jemima Scott wife of Joſeph Junʳ. July 31

1738

A Dead year not one owned

1739

93 Moſes Jewet }
94 Sarah Pickard }
95 Lydia Stickney } Jan. 14.
96 Eliſabeth Creſey }
97 Daniel Clark
98 Thomas Elsworth
99 Joſeph Kilborn } Feb. 11.
100 Jacob Smith
101 Stephen Palmer
102 Caleb Jewet April 15.
103 Jane Palmer
104 James Dickinſon April 29
105 Sarah Dole } May 6.
106 John Crosby June 10
107 John Osborn junʳ. Nov. 4,
108 David Dreiſer junʳ.

109 Samuel Cooper and
110 Mary his wife } Dec. 2.
111 Nathan Brocklebank Dec. 30
112 David Hammond junr. Feb.
113 Aaron Clark } Feb. 24
114 Jeremy Jewet Son of Aquila
115 Elisabeth Pickard datr. of Moses May 4.

1740

116 Kezia Dodge July 15.
117 Mary Pierson datr. of Stephen Sep. 14.
118 Thomas Johnson Feb. 8.

1741

119 James Hidden March 22
120 John Chaplin April 5
121 Elisabeth Boynton Deacons
    Grandatr.
122 Mary Brown Capt. Pickards } April 5.
    Grandatr.
123 Jane Northend
124 Mercy Gage
125 Jane Sanders
126 Phœbe Kilborn
127 Elizabeth Bennet June 7.
128 Nathanael Jewet junr. } June 14
129 Mary Kilborn

130 Benjamin Bishop
131 Moses Pickard junr. } July 12
132 Mary Todd datr. of John
133 Ebenezer Kilborn
134 Isaac Burpee
135 Mehetabel Roufe
136 Elisabeth little } July 26
137 Abigail Stowel
138 Frances Osborn
139 Sarah Osborn
140 Mary Hibbert
141 Jemima Bennet
142 Jeremiah Hopkinson junr.
143 Ann Jewet Aug. 9.
144 Elisabeth Palmer
145 Faith Jewet Sep. 6.
146 Elisabeth Dickinson
147 Sarah Crosbey Sep. 13.
148 Mercy Hopkinson
149 Jonathan Crosbey Oct. 25.
150 John Tenny
151 Joanna Blake Nov. 1.
152 Jemima Lufkirs
153 Mary Davis junr
154 John Bennet junr. } Nov. 15.
155 Moses Davis junr.
156 Mary Davis Tert.

157 Thomas Mighel
158 Jeremiah Burpee
159 Stephen Palmer jun.
160 Anne Galloway } Dec. 20.
161 Mofes Duty — Jan. 10.
162 Abigail Hunt — 24
163 Hannah Evans — Feb. 14.
164 Jeremy Elsworth jun.

1742

165 Joseph Barker } March 7
166 Mary Sanders
167 Abigail Jewet jun. } March 21
168 Hannah Crefey
169 Abigail Jewet wife of Mofes } April 4
170 Sarah Hammond
171 Lucy Pickard
172 Hannah Northend
173 Mofes Clark Son of Jonathan — Sep. 19
174 Mary Smith Dr. of Benja. — Jan. 30.

1743

175 John Todd jun.
176 Jeremy Mighil
177 Mary Jewet } April 17.
178 Margaret Wood

---

179 Hannah Dreiser
180 Rebekah King
181 Sarah Price } April 17.
182 Sarah Clark
183 David Pickard — Nov. 20.

1744

184 William Stickney — July 15
185 Thomas Hibbert — Sep. 2.
186 Hannah Day — Oct. 28.

1745

187 Elifabeth Barker — May 5.

1746

188 Edward Sanders jun. — June 7.

1747

189 Sarah Palmer Dr. of John — Oct. 18.

1748
1749

190 Prifcilla Jewet Dr. of Aquila — June 1749

The laft in the old Meeting-houfe

191 Jonathan Wood
192 Hannah Cooper } Oct. 29 the first in the new meeting-Houfe
193 Sarah Pearfon — 1750
194 Samuel Spiller — March 18
195 Mofes Bradftreet — July 1

No.	Name	Year	Date
196	Hannah Smith		Nov. 4.
197	John Johnfon		Jan. 27.
198	Elifabeth Mighil	1751	March 17
199	Edna Jewet		April 21.
200	John Palmer junr.		Aug. 4, 1751
201	Nathanael Gage	1752	Dec. 8.
202	Samuel Scot junr.		} June 14.
203	Bridget Scot his wife		
204	Hannah Jewet		June 28
205	Jofeph Smith		July 19.
206	William Price	1753	Oct. 1.
207	John Dickinfon junr.		June 3
208	Mofes Richards		July 29
209	Mehetabel Palmer	1754	Oct. 28
210	William Hobfon		April 21
211	John Hobfon		Sep. 22 1754
212	Samuel Wood		Oct. 27
213	William Todd		Nov. 3
214	John Palmer Tertius		Dec. 15
215	James Phillips	1755	Dec. 29
216	Nathanael Elsworth		} Feb. 16.
217	Hannah Harris		
218	Mary Payfon		March 9
219	Doctor William Hale		March 16
220	Samuel Pickard and		July 13
221	his wife		
222	The wife of Samll. Spiller		Nov. 2.
223	Mark Platts		Dec. 14.
	Thomas Todd and his wife		About Nov.
		1756	
224	Mary Platts wife of Samuel		Jan. 4.
225	Jofhua Jewet junr.		} Feb. 1.
226	Elifabeth Richards wife of Mofes		
227	Bridget Prime wife of Jofh.		} Feb. 22.
228	Mary Palmer wife of John junr.		
231	Nathan Dole		} March 14
232	and Phoebe his wife		
233	William Bayley		
234	Eliphalet Tenney		March 21
235	Francis Pickard junr.		} April —
236	Abigail Kilborn		
237	Oliver Hammond		Oct. 24.
238	Peter Cooper	1757	December 5
239	Mark Crefey		July 17
240	James Payfon	1758	Aug. 14.
241	Mofes Hopkinfon		} Feb. 19
242	James Todd		April 2d

243	John Dreiser	May 21
244	Amos Parsons	Sep. 3.
245	Joanna Parsons w. of Amos	Oct. 8.
	1759	
246	Paul Lancaster	Jan. 21
247	Widow Sarah Hammond	Feb. 4.
248	Jonathan Stickney &	} Feb. 18
249	Martha his wife	
250	Moses Stickney &	} April 15
251	Sarah his wife	
252	Mary Lancaster w. of Paul	June 8
253	Rebekah Parsons w. of Andrew	Aug. 5
	1760	
254	Price Hidden &	} Feb. 10
255	Eunice his wife	
256	Edward Payson junr	June 22
257	Paul Jewett and	} July 13
258	Jane his wife	
259	Hannah Hidden wife of Ephraim	July 20.
260	Widow Mary Cooper	Oct. 6.
261	Humphrey Sanders &	} Oct. 19
262	Jane his wife	
263	Dorothy Kilborn wife of Joseph	Nov. 23
264	Doctor Mark Howe	} Dec. 14.
265	& Mary his wife	
	1761	
266	Ephraim Hidden	} April 19
267	Daniel Dreiser junr.	
268	Anne Todd w. of James	June 7.
269	William Rutherford	
270	Mary Payson w. of Eliot junr.	Aug. 16.
271	James Cooper	Sep. 6.
272	Samuel Pearson &	} Sep. 13
273	Elisabeth his wife	
274	Benjamin Winter	Oct. 11.
275	Mary his wife — Sometime the Summer past	
276	Doctr. Nathaniel Cogswell	} Nov. 1.
277	& Sarah his wife	
278	Francis Palmer junr. &	} Nov. 29.
279	Rebecca his wife	
	1762	
274	William Sanders	March 28
275	Anne Sanders wife of William	April 4
276	Martha Hale wife of Doctor	April 25
277	David Stickney &	} Nov. 14.
278	Elisabeth his wife	
279	Mary Brown wife of Francis	
280	Jacob Pickard and	} Dec. 5
281	Salome his wife	
	1763	
282	Thomas Barker	} Feb. 13.
283	and his wife	

284 Stewart Hunt
285 and Edna his wife } March 20

286 Nathanael Bradstreet
287 and Phœbe his wife } July 10.

288 the wife of John Johnson   Sep. 18.

289 Sarah Bagley   Nov. 13

290 James Cresey and
291 Sarah his wife } Nov. 20.

292 John Sanders
293 & his wife } Dec. 11.

1764

294 Abel Cresey Junr.   April 15

295 Elisabeth Little
296 Lydia Hobson
297 Hannah Hobson } May 6.

298 Hannah Elsworth
299 Stephen Jewett junr. } May 20.

300 Nathan Pearson
301 Ezekiel Bayley
302 John Bradstreet } June 3d

303 Betty Lowel
304 Eunice Wood
305 Hannah Pickard } June 17

306 Eunice Duty
307 Jane Pickard
308 Sarah Dresser } Aug. 19

309 Elisabeth Gage   Aug. 26
310 Mehetabel Dresser   Sep. 16
311 Samuel Palmer   Nov. 25
312 John Pearson junr.   Dec. 2.

1765

Abel Bagley March 10   March 10
318 Anne Palmer w. of Samuel

314 Ezekiel Sawyer junr.
315 and Mary his wife } March 17

316 Hannah Payson   March 24

317 Mehetabel Dickinson w. of John jun.   April 14

318 Moses Lowel &
319 Mary his wife } June 16

320 Rebekah Burpee   Aug. 25.

321 David Hobson   Sep. 29

1766

322 Purchase Jewett junr. &
323 Sarah his wife } Jan 26

324 John Cresey   Feb. 9.

325 John Harris   March 16.

326 Timothy Harris and
327 Eunice Harris his wife } March 23

328 David Todd &
329 Sarah his wife } Sep. 28

1767

330 Aſa Todd	April 5
331 Joſeph Jewett	April 26
332 Daniel Kilborn	Aug. 9.
333 Nehemiah Jewett in Ipswich	
334 And his wife	Dec. 6.
335 Nathaniel Barker &	
336 Jane his wife	

1768

377 Joſhua Pickard	Jan. 3ᵈ.
378 Moſes Dickinſon	May 8
379 Hannah Todd wife of John the 3ᵈ.	June 26
380 Lydia Lancaſter	Aug. 21.
381 Nehemiah Jewett and	
382 Joanna his wife	Oct. 16.

1769

383 Benjamin Tenny	Jan. 1.
384 And Jane his wife	
385 Hannah Dickinſon daʳ. of Thoˢ.	March 12
386 Moſes-Paul Payſon	
387 And Deborah his wife	March 26
388 Moſes Scott and	
389 Mary his wife	Sep. 24.

1770

390 John Perley	Jan 14
391 Hannah Jewett daʳ. of Eliphalet	Mar. 4

392 Amos Bayley and	April 8.
393 his wife	
394 John Sawyer	July 8
395 Aaron Jewett	
396 Joſeph Kilborn junʳ.	July 29.
397 And his wife	Aug. 19.
398 Eliſabeth Sawyer wife of John	Feb. 9
399 Lydia Green wife of Thomas	
400 Widow Eliſabeth Kilborn	
401 Daniel Todd junʳ. and	May 12
402 Jane his wife	
403 Nelſon Todd and	Dec. 29.
404 His wife	
405 George Jewett junʳ.	
406 and his wife Sarah	

1772

407 Ephraim Jewett	Feb. 23.
408 Moſes Sawyer	May 17
409 Thomas Lambert junʳ. &	May 31
410 Apphia his wife	
411 David Jewett	Oct. 25
412 and his wife	
413 Thomas Elsworth junʳ.	Nov. 29
414 And Lucey his wife	

1773

415 Jacob Jewett junʳ.	Mar. 28 1773
416 And Eliſabeth his wife	

417 Ephraim Pickard
418 And his wife   } April 11.
419 Ezekiel Bradftreet
420 and his wife Abigail   } June 13
421 Mofes Jewett junr. and
422 Elifabeth his wife   } Nov. 7.

1774

423 William Gage and
424 Hannah his wife   } March 27
425 Sarah Jewett wife of Ephraim
    Thomas Mighill   recorder

1 Benjamin Todd and
2 Elifabeth His wife   } May 29 1774
3 Samuel-Northend Gage
4 and Lucy His wife   } June 19

5 Nathan Lambert
6 and Abigail his wife
7 Mofes Bradstreet junr.   } Octr. 15th 1775
8 and Sarah his wife
    Joseph Scott   the Churches Clerk
Solomon Lowell and his wife   feb. 1776
Nathan Todd   feb. 1777
    Those who have owned the Covenant

1778

Thomas Prime and
Mary his wife   } August 30th
Edward Bifhop and
Anne his wife   } Nov. 26
George Todd & Lucy his wife   } Decr. 12th
John Kilborn   March 4th 1781
Mary Kilborn w. of John   April 22 1781
[The end of Covenanters]

(To be continued.)

EARLY RECORDS OF ROWLEY, MASS.

(Continued from Vol. XXXIV, p. 116.)

BY GEORGE B. BLODGETTE.

A Record of perfons Baptized in yᵉ church at Rowley [Recorded by the Revᵈ. Samuel Phillips *second* minister]

	Time
Anthony Auftin his fon Richard	} Decemb: 3. 1665[1]
John Symons's daughter Elizabeth	
John Tod, his fon Thomas	Dec: 10. 1665
Sarah Tenny. Daughter of { John, Mercy	} Januvy: 8. 1665⁶
Elizabeth Hidden. Daughtr of { Andrew, Sarah	March. 25. 1666
Jane Pickard. Daughter of { John, Jane	} April 22. 1666
Sarah Pearson Daughter of John	June (3) 1666
Samuel Hones f. of { Richard, Alice	} June. 24. 1666
Mary Borebanke d: of { John	
Mary Remington. d. of { Thomas, Mehitabel	} Aug. 29. 1666

[1]If any record of Baptisms was made from 1659 to 1665 it ha been lost.

Thomas Jewet. f. of { Ezekiel, ffayth	} Octo: 28. 1666
Sarah Brocklebank. d. of { Samuel, Hannah	} Novem: 4. 1666
Ezekiel Northerne. f. of { Ezekiel, Ednah	
Samuel Wood. f. of { Thomas, Mary	} Decem: 30. 1666
Dorcas Phillips. d. of { Samuel, Sarah	} January. 6. 1666
Mary Symmonds d of { John, Elizabeth	} Aprill 7. 1667
Efther Hopkinsfon d. of { Jonathan, Esther	} April. 14 1667.
[One name gone]	
John Trumble.[2] f. of { John, Deborah	} May 12. 1667
Nathaniel Crofby[2] f. of { Antony, Prudence	} June. 23. 1667
Edna Hafun. d of { Edward, Hannah	} June. 23. 1667

[2] Dead.

(103)

Aquila Law f. of	{ William / ffayth }	July. 28. 1667
Samuel Shepard f. of	{ Samuel / Dorothy }	Aug: 25. 1667
Mary Dreffer. d of	{ John / Mary }	Sept. 1. 1667
Nathaniel Weft f. of	{ Twiford }	Oct. 13. 1667
Sarah Stickney d. of	{ Samuel / Julian }	Nov: 10. 1667
Jonathan Barker f. of	{ Barzilai / Anna }	
Jonathan Nelfon, f. of	{ Thomas / Anne }	Nov: 24. 1667
Anthony Auftin f. of	{ Anthony }	January. 19.1667
Mary Phillips. d. of	{ Samuel / Sarah }	Febr: 22. 1667
Thomas Longhorn f.of	{ Richard }	March. 29. 1667
Mary Weicom d of	{ Mary / Daniel / Mary }	April 19 1668
Mary Hopkinfon d of	{ Jonathan / Ester }	May 10 1668
Mary Barker d of	{ James / Mary }	May 31. 1668

Sarah Brocklebank d. of	{ Samuel / Hannah }	July 12 1668
Timothy Homes		July 26 1668
Ann Hidden		July 26 1668
of { abrahaan / An } Jewitt	{ Deborah / An }	Aug 9. 1668
of { Jonathan / Elizabeth } Platts	{ John / Jonathan / Jonas / Elizabeth }	Aug 9 1668
Br Tod his son Timothy		Aug: 23 1668
of { Ezekiel } Jewit his son	Ezekiel	Septemb:6. 1668
Br John Watfon daughter Hannah		Decemb 27 (68)
Goodm Simmons daughter Jane		March 21 69
Mehitabel Remington	T Adn 22	
a married woman	16.	
And her child Sarah		April 4 1669
Tobiah Coleman his son Jabez		April 25 1669
of { Abraham / An } Jewitt	{ William }	May 30. 1669
Goodm. Dickefons daughter Mercy		June 20 1669
Solomon Wood		June 27 1669
Mrs Crofby her child Nathaniel		July 18 1669
Br Hafen Richard		
Sister Hopkinfon Mary		Septemb 12 69

Ezekiel Jewitt his son Ezekiel	Octob 31 69
Ezekiel Northen his daght Mary	Novemb 25 69
Barzillai Barker Ebenezer	Decemb 26 69
Mr Tho: Nelson daughter Elizabeth	ffeb 27 69
Moses Bradstreet his son Umphrey	ffeb 27 69
Br Pickard daught Hannah	1670
Joseph Boynton his s. Joseph	May 22 1670
John Jackson his son John	June 19 1670
Jonathan Platts his son James	July 31 1670
Br Tod hi son Samuel	July 31: 70
Tobiah Coleman daughter Sarah	
Goodm Wheeler { son Joseph / daught Mary }	Sept: 4 1670
Goodm Bayly Junior his son John	Sept 11. 1670
Andrew Hidden his son Andrew	Octob. 23 (70
Samuel Phillips his son John	Octob 30 1670
Samuel Dreser daughter Mary	Novemb 20 (70
Mr Nelson Jerimiah	
John Jewitt Abigail } all baptized	Novemb 27 1670
Joseph Trumble John }	
Nathaniel Harrice his son Nathaniel	Jan 15 1670
Decon Brottibank daughter Jane	ffeb 5 1670
Thomas Lambert daughter Mary	ffeb 12 70
Timothy Palmer daughter Elizabeth	April 30 71
Goodm Borebank junr son Caleb	May 7: 1671
Jachen Reyner = Edward	
John Trumbl = Deborah }	July 2 1671

Br Johnson son Samuel	Aug 13 1671
Abraham Jewet daughter Mary	Aug 20 1671
John Dreser Junr daugh Martha	Aug 27 1671
Anthony Austin son John	Octob 29. 1671
John Watson son John	Novemb 19. 1671
William Foster son Timmothy }	
Samuel Dreser d. Elizabeth }	Decemb 10 1671
Samuel Peirson d. Mercy	
	1671
Br Hasen d. Hephzibah	Decemb 24 71
Br Wood Ebenezer son	Decemb 31 (71
Sister Hidden son Joseph }	
Barzillai Barker d. Hannah	Jan 7: 1671
Moses Bradstreets son Nathaniel	Jan 14 1671
Mr Nelson daughter Elizabeth	Jan 28 71
Goody Henning s. Shubael }	
James Barker d. Sarah }	ffeb 4 1671
Br Tod his son James	
Br Woodin daugh Dorcas }	ffeb 11 71
Br Ezeck Jewitt s. Maximi	
Joseph Bointon his d. Sarah	ffeb 18 71
Jonathan Hopkinson son Jerimiah	ffeb 25 71
	1672
John Peirson daughter Sarah	April 7
Goodm Bufwell daught Sarah }	
Goodm Coleman son Thomas }	April 28.

Samuel Dreſer son Samuel	Aug 31 1673
Mr Neh Jewitt daught: Mary	Septemb 7 1673
Goodman Elethrop dugh. Margeret	
Br Haſen Daughter Sarah	Septemb 21 73
Br Ezeck Jewitt daugh: Ann	Octob. 5, 1673
Moſes Bradſtreet daught Hannah	Novemb 9 1673
Tho Leaver daughter Sarah	
John Hopkinſon son John	Nov. 16 1673
Jer: Jewit his sons { Jer / Joseph / Thomas / Eleaser } daughter Sarah	Noveb 23 1673
Goodm Fosters daughtr Hannah	Nov 23 73
Goodm Lyons Junior daugh Sarah	ffeb 8 1673
Goodm Weicom John daugh Ann	April 5. 1674
John Trumbl daughter Mary	April 5 74
Saml Palmer d. Mary	May — 74
Goodm Haſletine John's son : a daugh. Elizabeth	June 14 1674
John Bill his d Ann	June 21 74
Br Wood his son James	
John Dreiſer son Jonathan	June 28 74
Nathaniel Barker son Nathan	Aug 23 74
Br Buſwel son Joseph	
Br Haſletine son Robert	Octob. 25 74

Br Abraham Hasletine d: Mary	May 5
Joseph Bayly daugh. Abigail	May 12
Nathaniel Barker d. Elizabeth	
James Dickeſon son John	June 2.
Daniel Weicom son Thomas	July 14
Sister Horfleek daugh Elizabeth	Jully 21
Br Remington son Samuel	July 28
John Simmons daught Sarah	Aug. 4
this day sister Harrice buried	
Goodm: Foster son Ebenezer	Aug 18.
Samuel Palmer daught Mary	
Samuel Haſletine d Deborah	Sept. 29.
Mr Thomas Nelſon son Gershome	Octob. 6
John Jewitt son John	
Nathaniel Harric daugh Bridget	Jan 12 72 / March 2 1673
Abel Platts son Moses	March 30 73
John Bayly daughter Ann	April 13 73
Joseph Chaplin son Joseph	April 27 73
Caleb Borebank son John	
Mr Philip Nelſon daught. Sarah	June 8 73
Joseph Trumbl daughtr Hannah	
Thomas Lambert daughter Rebeckah	June 15, 1673
Jonathan Platts son Isaack	June 22 1673
Joseph Bointon daughter Ann	
Caleb Bointon son William	
Goodman Hidden son Samuel	Aug: 24 1673

Joseph Chaplin son John	Nov 1 74
Mr Nelſon son Jeremiah	} Novemb 15 74
James Juitᵗ daughter Mary	
Captain Brotlebank son Joseph	Novemb 29 74
John Peirſon Junior son John	Decemb : 6 74
	1675
Br Woodin son Peter	March 14
Jer Jewitt daught Mary	
Tim Palmer son Timothy	} March 21
John Sawyer son Edward	
Joseph Trumble d : Mary	March 28
John Bayly s. Nathaniel	
Sam : Stickney s. William	} Aprill. 4
Daniel Weicom d. Francis	
Able Platts son Abel	June. 13.
Abraham Jewitt son Abraham	
Thomas Ally son Samuel	} July 4
ffayth Swans son Richard	July 18
Nathaniel Harrice d'Elizabeth	Aug 1
Moſes Bradſtreet son Samuel	Aug 22
[name torn off]	
Nehemiah Jewit son Thomas	Septemb 5
John Clark daughter Sarah	Septemb 12

¹ This is Chute. She was born 16 Sept, 1674, probably in Ipswich.

Goodman Chapman Dorothy	} Octob 10
Caleb Bointon Hannah	Octob 17
Caleb Borebank d. Mary	} Octob 24
Abraham Foster d Mehitable	
Br Birkby daughter Mary	Novemb : 7
Joseph Bointon son Richard	} Novemb : 28
Joseph Bayly son Richard	
Ezeck Jewit daught Sarah	Decemb 11
Br Langly daugh. Sarah	January 2
Samuel Lions son Samuel	January 9
Mr Jer : Shepard d. Hannah	
Samuel Prime son Samuel	
James Dickeſon d. Mary	ffeb. 6
Matthew Harriman d. Elizabeth	ffeb 20
Mr Tho Nelson d. Frances	
Tho : Pearly { s Thomas, d Liddeah, s Jacob	} ffeb 27
	1676
Br Tho Lambert son Nathan	March 5
Samuel Dreiſer son John	
Caleb Bointon son John	} April 9
Good. Herden son Ebenezer	
Jonathan Platts daugh Haħah	Aprill 15
Jonathan Hopkinſon son Jonathan	May 14
John Weicom daugh : Abigall	May 21

Benjamin Scott daugh Sarah	Septemb 9
Samuel Spafford son Samuel	Septemb 16
Br John Bayly son Thomas	Octob 21
Br Brown grandchild daught Sarah	}
John Peirson son Joseph	} Novemb. 4
Caleb Bointon daughter Margeret	
John Acye daughter Mary	
Mr Philip Nelſon daughter Martha	December 2
John Weicom son John	
John Clark son Richard	Decemb 9
William Foſter son Caleb	Decemb 23
Mr Shepard son Jeremiah	January 20
Jonathan Hopkinſon daugh Ann	ffeb 24
	1678
Caleb Borebank son Timothy	March 10
Daniel Weicom d. Rebeccah	March 31
Br Ezekiel Jewitt d : Elizabeth	Aprill 7
Br Tho : Lambert son Thomas	
B Tho : Pearly daugh Hephzibah	}
John Dreſſer daughter Sarah	} Aprill 14
Joseph Bointon son John	
Samuel Prime daught. Sarah	May. 12
Samuel Dreſſer son Thomas	June. 16
John Spafford his son John	June. 30
Mr Richard Dumer junʳ his son Richard	July 28
Jachin Rayner daugh Hannah	July 28

John Dreſſer daught Jane	June 4
Samuel Haſletine of Bradford s. Samuel	} July 9
Br John Trumble his son Judah	August. 6.
Couſin Mr Richard Dumer son John	August 20 :
Mathew Harriman son Mathew	Septemb : 24
Siſter Wheeler her son David	Octob 1
Br Foſter his son Samuel	Octob 29
Moſes Bradſtreet daughter Bridgett	Decemh 3
Barzillai Barker son Ezra	December 3
Nathaniel Barker son Jacob	January 21
John Sawyer daughter Mary	January 28
John Hopkinſon daughter Dorcas	ffebr : 25
	1677
Joseph Chaplin son Jonathan	Aprill 15
Br Langly son Abl	Aprill 29
Samuel palmer daught Martha	}
Samuel Peirson daught Elizabeth	} May 13
Mr Neh Jewitt daugh Joanna	}
Samuel Stickney son Thomas	} June 3
John Bointon son Iccabod	
Br Boſwell daughter Mary	July 8
Nathaniel Harrie S. John	July 15
Goodm : Allin son Stilſaʒ	
Tho : Leaver junior daughter Damaris	August 5
Br Coleby daughter Dorothy	Septemb. 2

Mathew Harrimon daughter Hannah	August 4
John Sawyer son Ezeckiel	August 11
James Dickinson son James	
John Bointon daughter Jane	August 18
Samuel Smith daugh Mary	
Tho: Alley daughter Sarah	Octob 6
Goodm Palmer son John	Decemb. 15
John Hopkinson son Jeremiah	Decemb 29
Able Platts daughter Hannah	ffeb.23

1679

Br Caleb Bointon daught. Ann	March 9
Joseph Jewitt son Jonathan	March 16
Barzillai Barker daught. Esther	March
Nathaniel Elethorp daugh Abigail	[torn off]
John Dreiser son Richard	June 29
Joshuah Bointon son Joshuah	July 6
Br Nathaniel Barker daugh Mary	July 13
Nathaniel Harrice daughter Hannah	July 27
Good Hardy deacon young son in law a son Samuel	
Mr Neh. Jewett son Nathan	Sept 7
John Clark son John	Octob 26
Mofes Bradftreet son Aaron	Novemb: 30
John Weicom daugh: Mary	January 18
Br Joseph Bointon s. Jonathan	ffeb 29

1680

Samuel Dreiser son Joseph	March 21
Caleb Borebank daughter Martha	March 28
Samuel Stickney son Jonathan	April 11
Br John Bayly son James	April 18
Br Thom Lamber daugh. Rebeckah	April 25
James Scales son James	
John Peirson junior daugh. Dorcas	May 2
Goodman Kimbal at Village-d: Elizab. May 9.	
Daniel Weicom daughter Martha	May 30
Abraham Jewit daughter Priscilla	June 6
yong Goodm Plumer Benjamin Son John	June 13
Goodm Wood of ye Village son John	June 20
Sifter Eftman of Salifbury son Zachery	
John Spafford daughter Mary ——	June 27
Goodm. ffofter daughter Ruth	July 18
Cousin Dummer son Richard	July 25
Joseph Chaplin son Jeremiah	August 1
John Sawyer daugh Elizabeth	August 15
Mr Philip Nelson daught. Ruth	August 29
Br Coleby son Isaack	Sept: 12
Goodm Allin, Salif-bury son William daughter Ann	Novemb 7 / Novemb 14
John Hobson son John	Novemb 14

Joseph Kilborn daughter Ann	Novemb 28
Mr Tho Hammond daughter Hannah	January 30
	1681
James Scales daughter Sarah	March 6
Samuel Prime son Mark	
Mr Neh: Jewitt daughter Mercy	March 13
Ephraim Dorman daught Hannah	March 20
Benjamin Scott son John	March 27
Ezeckiel Jewit son Nathaniel	
John Decker daughter Elizabeth	April 3
Benjamin Peirfon daught Hannah	
James Dickinfon son Samuel	April 17
Joseph Scott daughter Johannah	
Nathaniel Harric daugh Sarah	May 1
young Goodm Wallingford son Nicholas	May 22
Br Langly son John	July 10
Daniel Tenny son Thomas	July 17
James Baily son James	July 31
John Stickney Daughter Hannah	Aug 21
John Drefser son Nathaniel	Aug: 28
Joseph Scott Taylor daught Sarah	Sept 11
James Canady son James	Sept 25
Stephen Mighel son-in-law daught Sarah	Octob 23
Barzillai Barker daught: Ruth	Novemb 6

John Senter daugh Elizabeth	Novemb 13
Thom. Tenny Junior daughter Margeret	
Br Nathainel Barker daughter Johanna	Novemb 20
Br Caleb Bointon daughter Hephziba	Decemb 4
Br James Barker son Nathaniel	Decemb 11
Br Tho: Lambert son Nathan	January 22
John Wood daughter Hannah	
Jachin Reyner son Jachin	January 29
Caleb Bointon daughter Ruth	
John Clark son Judah	ffeb 12
Sam: Drefser daughter Hannah	ffeb 19
Able Platts son Samuel	
	1682
Br Joseph Bointon son Bennoni	March 12
Tho Lever Junior daughter Mary	
Mr Tho: Nelfon son Ephraim	March 26
John Spafford son David	April 2
Thom: Palmer capt son-in-law : son Sam:	April 9
Caleb Borebank son Eliezar	
Caleb Hopkinfon son Caleb	April 23
Benjamin Plumer son Benjamin	
Mofes Bradfreet son Samuel	May 14
William ffofter son Joseph	May 21
Cousin Mr Richard Dumer daugh. Elizabeth	July 23

Mr Simon Wainwright d Sarah — July 30
Benjamin Peirſon daughter Phebe — Sept. 3
Br John Sawyer son John ⎫
Siſter Kimbal Hannah ⎬ Septemb 10
Joseph Chaplin daughter Elizabeth ⎫
Samuel Spaſford daughter Sarah ⎬ Septemb. 24
Caleb Jackſon daughter Elizabeth — Octob 8
Benjamin Scot son Joseph — Octob 15
Goodm Decker son John ⎫
Good: Center son John ⎬ Octob 29
Samuel Brottlebanck son Samuel ⎫
Good Smith daughter Hannah ⎬
Jonathan Jackſon son Jonathan ⎬ Novemb 12
James Bayly daughter Elizabeth Mr ⎭
paiſon firſt he baptized — Novemb: 26
Mr Philip Nelſon son Joseph — Decemb 3
Jer: Peirſon d. Priſcilla — Decemb. 10
John Weicom daugh Mehitabel — Decemb 17
John Bayly daughter Mary — ffeb 4
Br Ezekiel Jewitt son Stephen — ffeb 25
James Scales son William — April 1 1683
Mr Neh: Jewit son Nehemiah — April 15
Br Coleby s. Abraham ⎫
Siſter Eſtman son Rob: ⎬ April 29
Br Trumble daughter Deborah — June 10
Samuel Prime daughter Ann — July 1

John Hopkinson daught Elizabeth — August 12
Joseph Jewitt son Joſhuah — August 26
Tho: Tenny Junior daughter Ann — Septemb 2
Abraham Jewitt daughter Elizabeth — Octob 7
Joſhuah Bointon son John — Octob: 28
Samuel Kilborn daughter Hannah — Novemb 18
Goodm Dorman { son Seth / daughter Phebe — Decemb 9
Samuel Dreſſer son Thomas ⎫
John Clark daugh Mary ⎬ ffeb 10
John Wood son John — ffeb 17

1684

James Dickenſon son George ⎫
Joseph Kilborn son Joseph ⎬ March 9
Nathaniel Harrice d: Jane — March 16
Br Nathaniel Barker d Mercy — March 23
young Goodm Plumer son Tho: — May 25
Br John Pickard son John — June 1
Dr Canada son John — June 8
John Stickney daught Elizabeth — June 15
Br S. Platts senior daughter Mary ⎫
Br Sawyer daughter Hannah ⎬ June 29
John Spaſford son Jonathan — July 6
Br John Dreſſer daught Liddiah ⎫
Son Mighell son Nathanl ⎬ July 20
Caleb Borebank son Samuel — Aug. 7

Br Joseph Bointon Jonathan — August 24
Br Peirson Junior daughter Jane — Aug. 31
Tho: Wood Junior daughtr Mary
Jonathan Jackson daughter Hannah — Sept 21
Br Joseph Jewitt son Aquilla
Br Samuel Brottlebank daughter Hannah — Sept 28
Br Sam: twins { son Thomas / daughter Phebe }
Palmer
Barzillai Barker Enoch
Cousin Mr Richard Dumer son Nathaniel — Octob 26
Mr Payson daughter Elizabeth — Nov: 9
Francis Palmer Junior daughter Elizabeth — Nov: 30
— Decemb 21

1685

Tho: Leaver daughter Liddeah — ffeb. 15
Goodm Hale Junior daughter Edna — ffeb. 22
Joseph Scott, Tayler son Joseph — March 15
Br James Scales son Mathew — March 29
Br Samuel Spafford daughter Hannah
Elizabeth Pearl daughter Eliz or — April 5
Samuel Dreser son Thomas
Benjamin Peirson son Daniel — April 12
Joseph Jewitt Br woods son-in-law daugh Hannah — April 26

Tho: Tenny Junior daughter Sarah
Joseph Jewitt daughter a twin Elizabeth — May 24
Jonathan Wheeler son Jonathan — July 19
Jer Pierson Daughter Miriam — August 2
James Tenny son James
Mrs Bennit { son David / son Spenier } — August 9
Stephen Peirson daughter Elizabeth — Aug: 30
Deaf lads¹ daughtr Elizabeth — Septemb 13
Mr Neh: Jewitt son Joseph — Septemb: 20
sister Lambert daughter Jane
Edward Hasen daughter Jane
Goodm [torn off] daughter Mary
Br John Bayley daugh. Elizabeth — Octob: 18
Br Caleb Bointon, Smith, son Jeremiah — Jan: 3
Goodm Tod Junior daughter Hannah — Jan: 17
Mr Paison daughter Sarah 2d daughter — Jan: 31
Br John Dreser daughter Elizabeth — ffeb: 20

1686

Son Mighell daughter Ann
James Bayly son John — March 19
Benjamin Scott son Benjamin — April 18
Br Clark Daughter Efter — April 25

¹ This means Isaac Kilborn who was deaf and dumb.

Joseph Kilborn son Georg	January 23
	1687
John Stickney daughter Mary	March
Barzillai Barker daugh Berthy	March
[two names torn off]	March 27
Joseph Jewett, s. to Br Wood, his son Joseph	Aprill 10
Tho Tenny junor daughter Elizabeth	May 1
John Spafford daughter Martha	
Stephen Peirfon son Stephen	June 19
Mofes Bradftreet son Samuel	
Samuel Dreffer son Jeremiah	July 3
ffrancis Palmer son John dead	
William Duty son William	July 10
Mrs Bennit son William	July 31
Br Joseph Jewitt daughter Prifcilla	August 14
Benjam: Peirfon daughter Ruth	
Caleb Borebanck son Ebenezer	Aug: 28
Samuel Kilborn son Samuel	Sept: 4
Josiah Wood son Joseph	Sept: 18
Mr Payfon daughter Mary	Sept: 25
Mr Tho: Crosby of Hampton son Anthony	Novemb 20
Br Joseph Bointon son Hilkiah	
Benjamin Scott son Benjamin	Novemb 27
Isaack Kilborn daughter Martha	

Timothy Harrice son Joseph	May 30
Mary Efinan of Salifbury daughter Elizabeth	
Cooper Palmer son Samuel	June 6
John Brown son Samuel	June 13
Jonathan Jackfon d. Liddeah	Auguft 1
Collen Frazer son Simon	August 8
Jonathan Harriman daugh Margaret	Aug 22
Goodm: Plummer daughter Sarah	Septemb 5
Br Brottlebank son John	Septemb 19
Tho: Wood junior Thomas	
Tobias Coleman daughter Judith	Octob 3
Goodwife Ayers Br Swans daught daughter Ruth	
Br Nathan: Barker son James	Octob 17
Captain Nelfon daughter Gemima	Octob. 24
Nathaniel Harris son Eliezer	Novemb 7
John Wood daughter Priscilla	
John Acle daughters 3 { Elizabeth, Hannah, Margeret }	Novemb 14
Richard Swan son Ebenezer	Decemb. 12
Mr Philip Nelfon Junior daughter Sarah	January 2
Mr Dummer son Shubael	January 16
Ezekiel Leiton son Richard	

Goodm Center Br Tods son in law daughter Eleaner	} Decemb 11
Samuel Bointon son Samuel	Jan : 8
Mr Neh Jewitt daughter Mehitabel	} ffeb 5
Br Samuel Spafford daughter Ruth	
Good Plummer—neck—daughter Abigail feb 26	

1688

John Hopkinſon daughter Ann	
James Bayly daughter Elizabeth	} March 11
Samuel Pickard son Samuel	
Colen ffracier son John	Aprill 1
Joseph Scott, Tayler son Ebenezer	Aprill: 15
John Tod junior son John	Aprill 22
Jer Peirſon daughter Hannah	Aprill 29
Br John Bayly daughter Liddeah	
Br Bointon, Smith, son Ebenezer	} [date effaced]
John Hidden son John	
Jonathan Wheeler daughter Mary	} June 10
Caleb Bointon Ipsw. daughter [effaced]	
Doctor Canada son Stephen	June 24
Nathaniel Brown son Nathaniel	
Thomas Wood son Nehemiah	
Anthony Bennitt daughter Rebeckah	} July 15
John Brown daughter Abigail	
Edward Haſen son Edward	July 22

Tho : Nelſon junior son Thomas	Auguſt 19
John Weicom daugh Sarah	
Jonathan Jackſon daught Mary	} Septemb. 2
Br Samuel Brottlebank dau : Sarah	Septemb 9
Dr Bennit daughter Sarah	Septemb 16
Benjamin Plumer son Stephen	
Timothy Harris daught Sarah	
Goodm West daughter Elizabeth	} Septemb 30
Br Dickenſon daughter Rebecah	
son Greenho daughter Elizabeth	} November 4
James Tenny daughter Abigail	Decemb 2
Captain Nelſon daughter Lucie	Decemb 16
Nathaniel Harrice son Edward	
Joseph Jewitt Junior daughter Sarah	} ffeb 10
Thomas Palmer son John	ffeb 17

1689

Br Clark son Ebenezer	
Samuel Bointon son Samuel	
Mihall Creaſy son Mighel	} March 3
Samuel Ayres son Stephen	March 17
Br Samuel Platts daughter Bethiah	March 24
Br John Peirſon junior daugh. Hepzibah	
Benjamin Peirſon daughter Abigall	} Aprill 14
William Duty daughter Sarah	
Moſes Bradſtreet daughter Elizabeth	} Aprill 21

Levtenant John Stickney son Samuel — March 30
Jer: Peirson son John — April6
Samuel Spofford son Samuel — April 27
Ezeck Leiton daughter Mary — June 15
Captain Bradstreet son Jonathan ⎫
John Spofford son Ebenezer ⎬ June 22
Goodman Pearl 2 daughters { Mary / Ellin } — July 13
John Brown daughter Mary ⎫
Mary Wheeler woman her child James ⎬ July 20
Joshuah Bointon { son Zachery / son William }
Br Elsworth daughter Sarah — July 27
Daniel Thofton junior son Daniel ⎫
Samuel Kilborn son David ⎬ Aug. 3
William Creasy son William ⎫
Philip Nelson son Philip / dau Sarah gemini ⎬ Aug 24
Benjamin Peirson son Benjamin ⎫
Nathaniel Brown son Nathaniel ⎬ Sept [torn off]
Goodman Searl son William
Antony Bennit son John
Joseph Plummer daughter Miriam — Octob 12
John Tod daughter Elizabeth — Novemb 2
Isaack Kilborn son Jacob — Novemb 9

Joseph Plumer son Moses ⎫
John Dresser junior daughter Abigail ⎬ May 5
Georg White sons { Nathaniel / Josiah } [torn off]
[torn off]
Stephen Peirson Daughter Martha ⎫ Jully 7
Colen ffrazier Daughter Elizabeth
Barzilla Barker son Noah — August 25
Mr Neh Jewitt daughter Mehitabell ⎫ Sept 22
Joseph Kilborn daught Mary
Joseph Bointon son Daniel
Samuel Dresser son Benjamin ⎫
Josiah Wood son Benjamin ⎬ Sept: 29
William Creasy daughter Ann — October 13
Br John Pickard son ffrancis ⎫
Ephraim Wood son [of] Thos Wood ⎬ Octobr 20
Benjamin Scott daughter Susanna
Richard Swan daughter Hannah ⎫ Nov: 3
Samuel Wood son Thomas — Nov. 10
Mr Paison son Eliphelet — Nov: 17
Samuel Pickard son Samuel — Decemb 8
Thom: Tenny daughter Hannah — ffeb 2

March 1690
Samuel Bointon Daughter Ellin — March 16

Timothy Harrice daught Phebe } Decemb 7
Mihal Creafy son Joseph
Thomas Aires son Jabez — Decemb 28
Mr Paifon daughter Mehitabel — January 25
Joseph Jewit merchant daughter Pricilla ffeb: 1
Mr Tho: Nelson junior son Samuel } ffeb 22
Stephen Peirfon daughter Mary

March 1691

Samuel Pickard son Thomas — March 15
John Heidden son Andrew
John Jewet { Dorcas { Rebeccah } Twins — March 22
Coufin Bayly son John — March 29
Goodman Plumer daughter An
Francis Palmer daughter Sarah } April 5
Widdow Downes Elizabeth &
her 2 children { Richard { Elizabeth } April 12
Jofeph Scott, Tayler daught. Sarah — Aprill 19
Daniel Weicom junior daught Mary — June 7
Goodm Duty son John — July 5
Jethro Wheeler daugh Hannah — July 26
Br Benj: Guttridg
sons { Samuel { John { Ebenezer } daugh { Sarah { Deborah } August 2

Br Clark son Jonathan — Sept 27
Mr Neh: Jewitt son Benjamin — Octob 4
Tho: Birkby junior son Jeremiah — Nov —
Jofiah Wood son Samuel — Nov 8
John Bradftreet son Mofes — Nov 15
John Dreffer junior daughter Lideah — Nov 22
Sarah Scales — widdow } Decemb 6
Mary Daniel — mayd } Decem —
Elizabeth Bennit mayd baptized
Benjamin Peirson daughter Sarah } Jan 24
Edward Hafen son John
Br John Pickard daughter Sarah }
Benjamin Scott son Samuel } Jan: 31
My son Samuel daughter Sarah }

1692

Tho: Dickenfon son John — March 13
Jonathan Jackfon son Jonathan — March 20
John Hopkinfon son John — April 3
James Tenny son John — April 10
John Peirfon daughter Rebeckah — April 24
Samuel Dreffer son Henery — May 1
John Weicom son Thomas
John Leiton son John
Jonathan Wheeler daughter Sarah } May 15
Samuel Cooper son Samuel }
Samuel Bointon son Daniel — May 29

Tho: Wood son Samuel	June 5
Jofeph Kilborn daughter Sarah	June 26
Jonathan Harriman son Jonathan	July 17
Samuel Silver daughter Mary	July 24
Samuel Spafford daughter Mary	Aug 14
Tho: Tenny son Samuel	Aug 21
Jethro Wheeler son Jethro	Aug 21
John Brown daughter Martha	Aug 28
Br Collen ffrazier daughter	Sept 9
Ezekiel Northen junior son John	Octob 16
Goodm: Elithorp, grandchild, daughter Sarah	Octob 23
Nathaniel Brown daughter Mary	Octob 30
Tho: Ayres son Abraham	Nov. 20
Jer Peirfon daughter Hephzibah	Decemb. 4
Mighel Creafy daughter	Decemb 11
Br Elfworth son Jeremiah	
Tho: Birkby daughter Sarah	Decemb 18
William Creafy son John	
Timmothy Harrice daughter Bridgett	Decemb 25
Mr Payfon son Samuel	
Levtenant Stickney daughter Sarah	ffeb 5
Tho: Jewitt s. Ezekiel	ffeb 19
Josiah Wood daughter Sarah	ffeb 19

Mr William Hobson son William	March 1693
Joseph Plumer son Aaron	March 12
Ipsw: Caleb Bointon daughter Mary	March 12
Br John Pickard son David	Aprill 9
Captain Jewitt daughter Johanna	Aprill 16
John Tod son Samuel	May 14
Br Nathaniel Barker son Nathaniel	June 11
Br Joseph Jewitt's daughter Rebecker	July 30
Hannah Bointon Samuel Bointon's wif batized	
Mary Silver Baptized	Octob. 8
and Mary Kirk eadem die	Octob 15
Stephen peirfon son Jonathan	Novemb 5
Samuel Cooper daughter Mary	Novemb 19
Ensigne Stickney son Andrew	Novemb 26
Br Bradftreet daughter Dorithy	Decemb 3
Joseph Bointon junior daughter Sarah	Decemb 10
Thomas Nelfon junior daughter Hannah	
Mr Ezeck Northen junior daughter Edna	Decemb 24
Samuel Ayers son Edward	January 14
John Platts daughter Mary	January 21
Cousin John Bradftreet daug: Elizabeth	January 28

Tho: Ayres son Tho:	Sept 16
Mr Nathaniel Crosby son Jonathan	
Mr Thomfon of Newberry daughter Abigail	Sept. 23
Samuell Bointon son Samuel	
Goodm Harriman son Leonard	Octob. 7
Goodm Ruffell son Jonathan	Octob 21
Nathaniel Harrice daughter Elizabeth	Nov. 4
Nathan Wheeler daughter Rebecker	
James Thurfton daughter Hannah	Nov. 18
Samuel Pickard son Mofes	Decemb 2
Br Tho: Jewet daughter ffayth	
Joseph Bointon junior son Nathaniel	Dec: 16
Jonathan Bayly son Jonathan	feb: 3
Jer: Peirfon daughter Miriam	feb: 10
Captain Jewitt son Jofhuah	feb. 17
Jonathan Look adult	
Benjam: Hazzen } twins	ffeb 24
Hephzibah Hazzen	
Jofhuah Bradstreet	
	1695
Francis Brotlebank } twins	
Elizabeth Brotlebank	March 3
Johanna Pickard	

Mr William Hobson daughter Ann	ffebe: 4
James Platts son Samuel	
Goodm: Duty son Mathew	
	March 1694
Ezekiel Leiton son Ezekiel	March 4
Tho: Birkby junior daughter Efter	March 11
Nathaniel Brown daughter Mary	March 25
Benjamin Peirfon son Jedediah	April 8
Tho: Wood daughter Elizabeth	
Mofes Bradftreet daughter Hannah	Aprill 22
Daniel Tenny } son Daniel } daughter Sarah	Aprill 29
Br John Brown son Samuel	
Samuel Silver daughter Elizabeth	May 6
James Bayly son James	May 13
francis Palmer son ffrancis	May 27
Mr Payfon son Edward	June 10
Samuel Spafford Abigail	
Collen ffrazier son John	June 17
Timothy Harrice daughter Dorcas	June 24
John Drefler junior daught Mehitable	July 8
Joseph Kilborn daughter Abigail	July 22
Daniel Weicom junior daught: Sarah	July 29
Mofes Platts son Able	Aug. 26
Br Benjamin Plummer daughter Mary	Sept. 2
Mr Philip Nelfon daughter Hannah	Sept. 9

Persons baptized beginning ye year 1696 whom I baptized; ye number taken from my day-book account

1696

189	Mercy Silver Dr Saml	March 15.
190	Bridget Bradstreet Dr Moses	March 22.
191	Lydia Platts Dr Moses Platts	April 5.
192	Shobael Bayley f. Jonathan	
193	Hannah Bointon Dr Joshua	April 19.
194	John Brown f. John	
195	Will. Look f. Jonathan	
196	Abigail Stewart Dr James	
197	James Platts f. John	April 26.
198	Benjamin Poor f. Henry	May 3.
199	Saml Duty f. William	
200	James Wood f. Ebenezer	
201	Peter Couper f. Saml	May 17.
202	David Plummer f. Joseph junr	May 24.
203	Abigail Kemball adult	june 7.
204	Saml Tod f. Saml Tod	
205	Rebeka Cole Mrs Bennets child	
206	Ebenezar ffrazer f. Collin	july 12.
207	Catherine Wentworth adult	Augst 2.
208	Maria Kilborn D Saml	Augst 30.
209	John Johnfon f. Saml	Septr 6.
210	Mercy Wheeler D. Nathan	Sept 13.

Purchas Jewit
Timothy Palmer—cooper— } April 7
Hannah Tenny
torn off
Tho: Dickenfon son Thomas — May 5
Aaaron Pengre daughter Rebeckeh }
Mighell Crefy son Jonathan — May 12 : 95
Jofiah Wood son James
Benjamin Peirfon daughter Mehit-able — June 23 1695

Samuel Ayres son Joseph — Auguft 4
Ezekiel Leiton : son Ezeck — Sept. 18
Goodm: Stephens son William — Septemb 29
William Hobfon daughter Sarah }
Tim: Harrice son John — Octob 13
Nathaniel Brown Martha daught. }
John Leiton daughter Martha — Octob: 20
Mr Jewtl daught. Ruth — Nov: 10
Tho: Tenny daughter Ruth — Nov: 17
Thomas Wood daught Mehitabel — Decemb 22
Andrew Stickney junior daught Rebeckeh — Decemb 29

[Recorded by the Revd Edward Payson fourth minister]

1This is Chute. She was born 2 Nov., 1695.

211	Mary Greenough Dr Robt	Septr 20.
212	Mary Tod Dr John	Septr 27.
213	John Tenney f. Danll	Octobr 18.
214	Mary Crefie D Will.	Novbr 8.
215	Eleazar Bointon f. Samll	Novbr 15.
216	Jane Stickney D. Jno	decembr 27.
217	Dorcas Thurston D. James	janry 3.
218	Nathanael Harriman f. Jonath.	janry 17.
219	Sarah Bradfireet D Humphy	
220	Mary Weicom D. Danll junr	

1697

221	Elifabeth Paifon my Dr	ffebry 7.
222	Hannah Bradftreet Dr Jno	ffeb. 14
223	Abigail Nelfon Dr Tho junr	
224	Ezeckll Northend f. Ezekll junr	March 7
225	Samll Jackfon f. Jonathan	
226	William Stevens adult	March 21
227	Mary Kilborn D Isaac	March 28
228	Mofes Peirfon s. Jeremiah	
229	John Dreifer f. Jno junr	April 11
230	Martha Plumer D. Benja	
231	Mehetabel Aiers D. Thomas	April 25
232	Elifabeth Pickard D. Samll	
233	Jeremiah Hopkinfon f. Michael	May 9

234	William Wentworth	The children
235	Sylvanus Wentworth	of
—	Paul Wentworth	PaulWentworth
—	Ebenezar Wentworth	May 16
—	Aaron Wentworth	1697
—	Mofes Wentworth	
240	Martha Wentworth	
—	Mercy Wentworth	
—	Mary Wentworth	
243	Catherine Wentworth	
244	Sarah Wentworth	
245	John Plumr f. Jonathan	
246	Sarah Brown D Nathll	june 6
—	Hannah Wheeler D Jethro	jun 13
248	Simon Pickard f. Jno	July 18
—	Patienc Peirfon D. Stephen	Augst 1
250	Elifabeth Crofbie D Nathll	Augst 8
251	Gerfhom ffrazer f. Colin	Augst 15
252	Daniel Lunt f. John	Augst 22
253	Jeremiah Hobfon f. Will.	Septr 12
254	Bridget Bointon D. Jofeph junr	Octobr 10

This was ye last child baptized in the old meeting-houfe. Which house we left, & went to worfhip God in our new houfe Nov. 7, 1697

1698 2nd Meet. house

255	Amos Stickney f. Andrew	Janry 2

This was ye firft child that was baptized in or new meeting-houfe

256 Tamer Crecie D. Michael — ffeb. 6
257 Mofes Bradftreet f. Mofes — ffebry 27
258 Ruth Silver Dr Samll — March 6
259 Mary Harris D. Timothy — March 13
260 Ebenezar Burtbe f. Thomas — April 3
261 Mehetabel Jewett D. Thomas — April 3
262 Sarah Look D. Jonathan — Aprill 3
263 Ebenezar Wheeler f. Jonathan Gemini — April 20
264 Mehetabel Wheeler D. Jona-than — April 20

baptized at his own houfe becaufe one of ym was nigh its end in appearanc. yr were prefent 7 of ye chh. in full comunion & two more honeft neighbours &c.

265 Mehetable Spoford D. Samll — May 1
266 Jofeph Brown f. John — May 8
267 Elifabeth Pore D. Henry — May 22
268 Job Harris f. Nathll
269 Gerfhom Tenney f. James — May 29
270 Mary Platts D. James — June 19
271 Nathan Platts f. Samll — june 26
272 John Bayley f Jonathan
273 Jane Pickard D. Widow — july 3

274 Samuel Hazen f. Edward — july 24
275 Solomon Stewart f. James
276 Jonathan Hopkinfon f. Michael — July 31
277 Mary Pickard D. Samuel Pickard — August 28
278 Elifabeth Davis D. Cornelious Davis — Septembr 11
279 Andrew Deuty f. William Duty — Septembr 18
280 Hannah Paifon my Dr
281 John Weft f. John — October 16
282 Mary Lunt Dr John
283 William Tenney f. Danll — Octobr 30
283 John Syle f. Richard — Novembr 6
284 Mary Harriman D Jonathan — Nover 13
285 Joseph Bointon f. Jofeph
286 Benjamin Brown f. Nathll — Novembr 20
287 Ebenezar Wood f. Ebenezar — Decembr 11
288 Benjamin Wentworth f. Paul — January 1
289 Hephzibah Peirfon D. Stephen — Janry 22
290 Mary Wood D. Jofiah — January 29
291 Isaac Jewett f. Isaac Ipfw.
292 Abigail Wheeler D. Nathan
293 Mehetabel Thurston D. Jofeph
294 Jofeph Thurston f. Jofeph — february 5
295 Benjamin Thurfton Gemini f. Jofeph

296	James Stewart	} Adult	
297	John Stewart	} Adult	
298	Rachel Wood		ffebʳuary 12
299	Eliſabeth Platts D. Moses		
300	Daniel Jackſon f. Jonathan		

Ma 1699

301	Joſeph Hedden f. Samuel	March 5
302	Hannah Welcom D Danˡˡ	March 12
303	Eliſabeth Geage D. Thomas senʳ	March 19
304	Jane Northend D. Ezekiel	
305	Hannah Creaſie D. William	Aprill 2
306	Hannah Jewet D. Maxˀmilian	April 9
307	Isaac Boynton S. Samuel	Aprill 16
308	Eliſabeth Dickinſon D. Thomas	Aprill 23
309	Thomas Tod f. John	
310	Abner Thurston f. James	Aprill 30
311	Jonathan Nelſon f. Thomas Junʳ	
312	Eliſabeth Nelſon D. John Nelſon	May 7
313	Jedidiah Kilborn s. Samuel Kilborn	May 28
314	Amos Stickney f. Andrew	June 4
315	Samuel Johnſon f. Samˡˡ	june 11
316	Mary Hobſon D. William	
317	Sarah Davis D. Cornelious	july 30

318	Mehetabel Tenney D. Thomas	August 27
319	Nathaniel Crosbie f. Nathaniel	September 10
320	Jeremiah Peirſon f. Jeremiah	
321	Sampſon Plummer f. Joſeph at yᵉ Neck	Septembʳ 17
322	James Dreſſer f. Jnᵒ junʳ	Octobʳ 1
323	Mary Stewart D. John	October 8
324	Nathan Phrazer f. Collin	January 14
325	John Stickney f. John	
326	Jonathan Burtby f. Thomas	January 28
327	Jonathan Peirſon f. Benjamin	
328	Hephziebah Jewett D. Thomas	ffebʳʸ 4

1700

329	Eliott Palſon my son	
330	Moſes Wheeler f. Jethro	
331	Hannah Walker D. Richard	March 17
332	Joſeph Pickard f. Samuell	March 24
333	John Geage f Thomas junʳ	Aprill 7
334	Ann Wood D. Thomas Wood	Aprill 14
335	John Bradſtreet f. Moſes	
336	Mary Tod D. James	Aprill 21
337	John Kilborn f. Isaac	May 12
338	Hannah Hardy Adult	
339	Moſes Hopkinſon f. Michael	June 9
340	Stephen Harris f. Timothy	
341	Hepizibah Hobson D. John	June 16

367	Dorothy Northend D. Ezekiel	} March 23
368	Sarah Harriman D Jonathan	
369	Mary Trumble D. Judah	
370	Andrew Stickney f. Andrew jun^r	March 30
371	Richard Tenney f. Daniel	Aprill 6
372	Nathan Drefser f. John jun^r	Aprill 13
373	Stephen Woodman f. Jonathan	} Aprill 20
374	Hannah Couper D. Samuel	
375	Abigail Creafie D. Michael	
376	Hephzibah Weicom D. Daniel	May 4th
377	Nathanel Nelfon f. Gerfhom	May 11
378	William Hobfon f. William	May 25
379	Sarah Drefser D. Sam^{ll} jun^r	June 8
380	Nathan Davis f. Cornelious	June 22
381	Stephen Bointon s. Sam^{ll}	July 20
382	Isreal Hazzen f. Edward	July 27
383	Nathan Wheeler f. Nathan	Augst 10
384	Dorothy Lunt D. John	} Augst 17
385	Samuel Jewett D. Daniel	
386	Thomas Tod f. John Tod	Augst 24
387	Margaret Elethorp D. Nathan^{ll} jun^r	Septr 21
388	Benjamin Stickney f. Benjamin	October 12
389	Jofeph Bayley f. Nathan^{ll}	October 19
390	Samuel Bayley f. James	} Novr 2
391	Jonathan Wood f. Ebenez^r	

342	Lidia Spoford D. Sam^{ll} Spoford	July 7
343	Abigail Pearley D. Samuel	} July 14
344	Abner Tod f. Samuel Tod	
345	Jonathan Drefser f. Jonathan	August 11
346	Hannah Chute D. James	} Augst 18
347	John Nelfon f. John	
348	Samuel Silver f. Samuel	
349	Edward Wentworth f. Paul	Augst 31
350	Mary Platts D. James	
351	Sarah Brown D. Nathan^{ll}	} Septemb^r 8
352	Hannah Plumer D. Jofeph	
353	Hannah Brown D. John	Septemb^r 22
354	Mofes Duty f. William	September 29
355	Samuel Wheeler f. Jonathan	
356	Abigail Thurfton D. Jofeph	} Octob^r 27
357	Daniel Pore f. Henry	
358	Benjamin Bointon f. Jofeph	Decemb^r 22
359	Abell Creafie f. William	December 29
360	Jofeph Jewett f. Jonathan	Jany 5
361	Stephen Paifon my son	
362	John Platts f. John	} Jany 26
363	Elifabeth Look D. Jonathan	ffeb^y 2
364	Ann Bayley D. Jonathan	ffeb^y 16
	1701	
365	Benjamin Stewart f. James	} March 9
366	Elifabeth Jewett D. Maxim.	

392	Tabitha Walker D. Richard	Nov. 26
393	Jonathan Burtbe f. Thomas	Novr 30
394	David Dickinfon f. Thomas	
395	Elifabeth Harris D. Timothy Harris	January 4th
396	Sarah Geage D. Thos Geage jun^r	
397	Amos Peirfon f. Jeremiah	January 11
398	Hannah Chaplin D. John & Margaret	ffeb^r 22

1702

399	Sarah Payfon my Daughter	March 8
400	Daniel Johnfon f. Samuel	March 15
401	Hester Tod D. James Tod	
402	Martha Dreifer D. John jun^r.	March 22
403	Elifabeth Hedden D. Ebenezer	March 29
404	Nathan Plummer f. Benjamin	April 12
405	Mehetabel Brown D. Nathaniel	April 26
406	Abigail ffrafier D. Collin	April 26
407	Dorothy Nelfon D. Tho. jun^r.	May 3
408	Deliverance Look D. Jn^oath.	
409	Mary Look D. Jona-than — Adult	May 17
410	John Peirfon f. Jofeph	

411	Mofes Scott f. John	May 31
412	Sarah Silver D. Sam^ll	June 7
413	Mary Lambert D. Thomas	June 28
414	Abijah Wheeler f. Jethro	July 5
415	Elifabeth Spoford D. Sam^ll.	
416	Sarah Jewett D. Thomas-Boxford—	July 12
417	Sarah Plummer D. Jofeph	July 19
418	Jonathan Dreifer f. Jonathan	July 26
419	Sufanna Tod D. Samuel	Septr. 27
420	Humphery Hobfon f. John	Octob^r. 4
421	David Pearley s. Samuel	Novemb^r. 1
422	Jonathan Nelfon f. Jeremiah	Novemb^r. 8
423	Hannah Platts D. Mofes	
424	David Bointon f. Richard	Novemb^r 15
425	Elifabeth Jewett D. John	Decemb^r 13
426	Benoni Bayley s. Jonathan	decemb^r 27
427	Patience Barker D. Jacob	Jan^ry 10
428	David Stewart f. James	
429	Hannah Northend D. Ezekiel	Jan^ry 31
430	Bridget Bointon D. Joseph	
431	Patience Walker D. Richard	ffeb^y 28
432	Hannah Thurfton D. Jofeph	

1703

433	Jonathan Payfon my son	March 7
434	Daniel Dreifer f. Samuel jun^r.	March 14

435	Benjamin Jewett f. Jonathan	Aprill 4
436	Jacob Wood f. Jofiah senr.	April 11
437	James Brown f. John	April 18
440[1]	Mofes Couper f. Samuel	April 25
441	Hannah Jackfon wife Jonath. Adult	May 2
442	Hannah Wood D. widow Wood	May 23
443	Elifabeth Broclebank D. Joseph	
444	Abigail Look D. Jonathan	Jun 6
445	Abigail Lunt D. John	
446	John Harriman f. Jonathan	Jun 13
447	Mofes Stickney f. Benjamin	June 20
448	Hannah Scott D. John	June 27
449	Sarah Jewett D. Daniel	July 4
450	David Plummer f. ffrancis	July 25
451	Ebenezer Tenny f. Danll.	Augst 15
452	James Platts f. James	Augst 15
453	Anne Nelson D. Gerfhorm	Sept. 5
454	Ruth Brown D. Nathanll.	Sept. 12
455	Sarah Hedden D. Ebenezer	Octobr 3
456	Nathanael Bayley f. Nathanll.	Octobr 31
457	Martha Hobfon D. William	Novbr 7
458	Abraham Bointon f. Samuel	Novbr 21
459	Solomon Nelfon f. ffrancis	
460	Hephzibah Platts D. John	Decembr 5
461	Daniel Elethorp f. Nathanll.	
462	Mary Dickinfon D. James	
463	Hannah Burthe D. Tho.	
464	Elifabeth Welcom D. Danll.	Decembr 19
465	Jemima Cheut D. Lionel	
466	Phinehas ffelt f.	Janry 9
467	Ruth Jewett D. Abraham	Janry 17
468	Jonathan Hopkinfon f. Michael	Janry 23
469	David Hale f. Jofeph	
470	Benjamin Tenney s James	
471	Thomas Lancafter f. Samll.	Janry 30
472	Jane Nelfon D. Jeremiah	
473	Abel Platts f. Mofes	ffebry 6

1704

474	Dorothy Rogers D. Robt	March 5
475	David Creafie f. Micheal	March 12
476	John Colman f. Thomas	Aprill 16
477	Jane Pickard D. Samuel	May 7
478	Moses Dreifer f. Jno. junr. 3s.	
479	Hannah Peirson D. Jeremiah	May 21
480	Debborah Plummer D. Jofeph	

[1] Error in original.

481	David Wood f. Ebenezer	
482	Hephzibah Pore D. Henry senr.	June 5
483	Jofhua Pore f. Henry junr.	
484	Jonathan Johnfon f. Joseph Haverhill.	June 18
485	Nathaniel Broadftreet f. Mofes	June 25
486	John Jewett f. John	
487	David Dreſser f. John junr.	July 23
488	Samuel Creafie f. William	
489	Sarah Wallingford D. Nicholas	
490	Mary Hedden D. Samuel	Augſt 18
491	Abigail Clark D. Richard	
492	Rebeka Walker D. Richard	
493	Sarah Lambert D. Thomas	Augſt 27
494	Abigail Plummer D. John	
495	Lawson Frazier fon Collin	Septr 10
496	Elifabeth Wheeler D. Nathan	Octobr 15
497	Seth Jewet f. Maximilian	
498	Elifabeth Nelfon D. Thomas	Octobr 22
499	Jofeph Tod f. John Tod	Octobr 29
500	Nathan Bointon f. Richard	
501	Mehetabel Woodman D. Jofhua	Novr 5
502	Thomas Dreſser f. Jonathan	
503	Hannah Harris D. Timothy	Novr 12
504	Hannah Johnfon D. Samuel	Decembr 24
505	Jonathan Tod f. James Tod	
506	Moses Hobfon f. John Hobfon	Decembr 31
507	Nathan Burtbe f. Thomas	
508	Hannah Hazzen D. Edward	Janry 14
509	Mary Dreſser D. Samuel junr.	ffebry 19

1705

510	Mehetabel Northend D. Ezekiel	March 4
511	David Payfon my son	March 11
512	Margaret Barker D. Jacob	March 18
513	Patience Pearley D. Samuel	March 25
514	Isreal Look f. Jonathan	
515	Jofeph Stickney f. Benjamin	
516	Mofes Geage f. Thomas	April 1
517	Mercy Chaplin D. Jeremiah	
518	Elifabeth Chaplin D. John	Aprill 8
519	Hannah Stewart D. James	Aprill 15
520	Mary Wheeler D. Jethro	April 22
521	Abiel Bointon s. Joseph & Bridget	April 29
522	Mercy Nelfon D. Francis & Mercy	May 20
523	Stephen Stickney f. Andrew	May 27
524	Jedidiah Jewett f. Jonathan	Jun 3
525	Richard Peirfon f. Jofeph	June 10
526	Jonathan Clark f. Judah	
527	Ednah Prime D. Mark	June 17
528	Mary Nelfon D. John Nelfon	June 24

529 William Jewet f. Aquila ⎱ July 15
530 Jofeph Deuty f. William ⎰ July 29
531 Abraham Brown f. John
532 Jofeph Jackfon f. Jonathan — Augst 27
533 Benjamin Thurfton f. Jofeph — Septr 2
534 Elifabeth Plummer D. John — Septr 16
535 Dorothy Hedden D. Ebenezer
536 Abigail Jewet D. Isaac ⎱ Septr 23
537 Hannah Platts D. Isaac
538 Mary Sawer D. Ezekiel junr. — Septr 30
539 William Brown f. Nathaniel — Octobr 14
540 Jofiah Bayley f. Nathaniel
541 Mary Tenney D. Daniel ⎱ Novembr 4
542 Samuel Harriman f. Jonathan — Novr 11
543 Nathanael Bradfreet f. Mofes — Novr 18
544 Hannah Trumble D. Judah — Decembr 23
545 Anne Jewet D. Abraham — Decembr 30
546 James Dickinfon f. James deceafd January 6
547 Hannah Pickard D. Samuel ⎱ ffebry 3
548 Sarah Dickinfon D. George
549 Dionyfius Rogers D. Robort — ffebry 24
550 Daniel Greenough f. Robert Junr March 3

1706

551 John Kinrick f. John — March 10
552 Mark Creafie f. William — March 24

553 Samuel Heydden f. Samuel — March 31
554 Caleb Hobfon f. William — April 7
555 Samuel Wood f. Ebenezar
556 Elifabeth Wood D. Jofiah
557 Mehetabel ffelt D. Samuel
558 Lydia Lancafter D. Samuel
559 John Clark f. Richard
560 Stephen Drefser f. John junr
561 Margaret Wallingfor D. Nicholas ⎱ July 14
562 Dorothy Woodman D. Jofhua
563 Samuel Pore f. Henry — Augst 18
564 Ebenezer Davis
565 Samuel Davis
    The children of John Davis
566 Sufannah Davis
567 Elifabeth Davis
568 Richard Walker f. Richard, Nubary — Octobr 13
569 Mary Mighel D. Nathanael
570 Sarah Brattlebank D. Samll jun
571 Eliphelet Kilborn f. Samuel ⎱ Octobr 20
572 Sarah Colman D. Thomas
573 Elifabeth Stewart D. James — Novr 10
574 Ann Lambert D. Thomas — Novr 17

575	Abraham Bointon } S^s Samuel }	Gemini Novr 24
576	Mofes Bointon	
577	Sarah Drefser D. Jonathan }	Decemb^r 8
578	Mehetabel Jewett D. Aquilla	
579	Samuel Northend s. Ezekiel	Jan^ry 19
580	John Hobson f. John	Jan^ry 26
581	Jonathan Chaplin f. Jeremiah	ffeb^ry 16
582	Mary Jewett D. Joseph jun^r	ffeb^ry 23

1707

583	Joseph Dickinfon f. Thomas	March 2
584	Sarah Bointon D. Benoni	March 9
585	Leonard Couper f. Samuel	March 16
586	Samuel Greenough s. Robt jun^r	March 30
587	Hannah Hopkinfon D. Jeremiah	April 6
588	Elifabeth Platts D. Ifaac	April 6
589	Mofes Platts S. Mofes	April 13
590	Philips Payton My son	April 27
591	Sarah Burtby D. Thomas }	May 25
592	Samuel Drefser s. Samuel	
593	Elifabeth Plummer D. Joseph	
594	Samuel Dickinfon S. Samuel }	June 1
595	Jane Drefser D. Joseph	
596	Ezekiel Sawer f. Ezekiel }	June 22
597	Sarah Hopkinfon D. Michael	

598	Jeremiah Nelfon s. Joseph }	Jun 29
599	Johannah Platts s. John	
600	Joseph Creafie s. William	July 6
601	Mercy Barker D. Jacob	July 27
602	Ephriam Bointon s. Joseph	Aug^st 3
603	George Dickinfon s. George	Aug^st 10
604	Daniel Jewet s. Daniel	
605	Mofes Tenney s. Thomas jun^r	Septr 14
606	Jane Prime D. Mark	
607	Hannah Clark D. Judah	
608	Mary Johnson D. Samuel	Septr 28
609	Mary Broclebank D. Joseph	
610	Mary Jewet wife Joseph Adult	Novr 16
611	David Bayley s. Nath^ll	
612	Georg Hybert Adult	
613	Prifcilla Jewett Adult	
614	William Jewett S. Abraham }	Novr 30
615	Sarah Jewett D Nathan^ll	
616	Stephen Mighel S. Nath^ll	
617	Samuel Prime S. Sam^ll	
618	Hannah Bointon D. Sam^ll }	Decemb^r 7
619	Sarah Wheeler D. Jethro	
620	David Jewett S. Isaac	Jan^ry 4
621	Jacob Jewet S. Jonathan	Jan^ry 25
622	Jane Bradftreet D. Mofes	ffeb^ry 1
623	Sarah Nelfon D. Gerfhom	ffeb^ry 15

1708

624	John Rogers S. Robert	March 7
625	Jeremiah Todd f. James	March 21
626	Mary Hedden D. Ebenezr	March 28
627	Rebekah Dreiser D. John	} May 16
628	Dorothy Bointon D. John	
629	Priscilla Todd D. Samuel	} June 20
630	Sarah Bointon D. Benoni	
631	Ellifabeth Jewett D. John	June 27
632	George Jewett S. Jofeph	Augst 1
633	George Wood S. Jofiah	Augst 15
634	Mofes Davis f. John	September 5
635	Mehetabel Scott D. John	Septr 26
636	Rebecca Bennet D. William Junr	Decembr 12
637	My deer Sarah Payfon, & severall more in the time of my sicknefs.	

1709

638	John Chaply fon John	Jun 12
639	Jeremiah Dreifer S. Jofeph	} July 3
640	Hannah Bayley D. Jonathan	
641	Sarah Smith D. Benjamin	Augst 14
642	Mary Chaplin D. Jeremiah	Augst 28
643	Sarah Geage D. William	
644	Tho: Tenney junr his Dr	
645	Richard Clark s. Richard	September 11

646	Lydia Pengry D. Aaron Junr	October 9
647	Abraham Bointon S. Saml	} Octobr 30
648	Jeremiah Jewett S. Nehemiah	
649	Phebe Jewett D. Stephen	Novr 6
650	Mercy Clark D. Judah	Novr 13
681	Samuel Bayley S. Nathll[1]	Novr 27
682	Jane Boynton D. Hilkiah	Novr 27
683	Mehetabel Chaplin D. John	Decembr 4
684	Mary Bointon D. John	Decembr 25
685	Mofes Broclebank s. Jofeph	Janry 15
686	Daniel Rogers S. Robert	Janry 22
687	David Dreifer S. Samuel	} ffebry 19
688	Samuel Searls S. John	

1710

689	Jonathan Johnfon S. Samuel	} April 2
690	Hannah Platts D. Mofes	
691	Zacheus Bointon S. Jofeph	} April 9
692	Stephen Bointon S. Benonl	
693	Ezekiel Mighel S. Nathll	May 21
694	Thomas Prime S. Mark	June 25
695	Sarah Platts D. James	} June 25
696	Jane Scott D. John	
697	Jewett D. Isaac	July 2
698	Mehetabel Jewett D Jonathan	July 23

[1] Mistake in original—dropping out 30 numbers.

699	Mark Prime S. Samuel	Augst 6
700	John Pickard s. Samuel	
701	Samuel Rofs S. Danll	Septr 3
702	Nathan Jewett S. Jofeph	Septr 10
703	Jofeph Smith S. John	September 17
704	Ezra Jewett S. Aquila	Octobr 15
705	Benjamin Sawyer S. Ezekiel	Novr 5
706	Elifabeth Northend D Lievt Ezekll	Decemr 17
707	Eben Hedden S. Ebenezer	
708	Hannah Lancaster D. Hannah	decembr 24
709	James Hybirt S. George	december 31
710	Stephen Hedden S. Samuel	
711	Rebecca Dickinfon D. George	January 7
712	Mehetabel Nelfon D. Ephraim	Janry 14
713	Sarah Bayley D. Jonathan	Janry 21
714	Mary Scott D. Jofeph	Janry 28
715	Amos Pilsberry s. Amos	
716	Sarah Pickard D. Jonathan	ffebry 11
717	Mehetabel Palmer D. Samuel	March 4
718	Jane Bridges D. John	March 11
	1711	
719	Hannah Barker D. Jacob	April 1
720	Mary Hopkinfon D. Jeremiah	
721	Mary Nelfon D. Gerfhom	April 8
722	Mofes Smith S. Benjamin	Jun 10

723	Richard Greenough Sons Robt Junr	July 22
724	Epps Greenough	July 29
725	Sarah Kilborn D. Jofeph	
726	Thomas Geage S. William	Augst 5
727	Thomas Clark S. Richard	
728	Mehetabel Todd D. James	
729	Thomas Lambert s. Thomas	
730	Hannah Drefser D. Jonathan	Augst 29
731	Mary Geage D. Thomas	
732	Hannah Drefser D. Jofeph	Septr 2
733	Judah Clark S. Judah	October 7
734	Mehetabel Chaplin D. Jeremiah	Octobr 14
735	Elifabeth Hodgkin D. John	Decembr 2
736	John Smith S. John	
737	Eliphalett Jewett S. Stephen	Janry 27
738	Stephen Pengry S. Aaron	
739	Elifabeth Searl D. John	
740	Birthiah Boīnton D. John	ffeb. 10
	1712	
741	Mary Pilberry D. Amos	March 2
742	Jofiah Jewett s. Jofeph	
743	Mercy Bayly D. Nathanll	March 23
744	Mofes Wood S. Ebenezer	
745	Elifabeth Tenny D. Tho Junr	April 6

746	Hannah Rogers D Robert	April 13
747	Benjamin Dow S. John	April 27
748	Sarah Stewart D. John	May 4
749	James Barker S. James	May 11
750	Hannah Petrſon D. Stephen	May 18
751	Mehetabel Dreſſer D. Samuel	Jun. 22
752	John Greenough S. Robert	July 27
753	Moſes Sawyer S. John	Augᵗ 3
754	Daniel Palmer S. John Palmer	Septemʳ 7
755	Jane Scott D. Joſeph	Septemʳ 14
756	Eliſabeth Jewett D. Aquilla	Septembʳ 21
757	Nathanel Plummer S. Joſeph	Sept 28
758	Edna Bointon D. Joſeph junʳ	October 5
759	Joshua Prime S. Samuel	Octob 19
760	Jane Sawyer D. Ezekiel	Novemb. 9
761	Mary Wood D. Thomas	Novʳ 16
762	Mehetabell Platts D. Moſes	
763	Suſanna Paiſon my daughter	Novʳ 23
764	Sarah Mighell D. Nathanᵘ	
765	Samuel Palmer S. Thomas	
766	Henry Elithorp an Adult man	Decembʳ 7
767	John Chaplin S. John	January 11
768	Mark Jewet s. Jonathan Jewett	January 18
769	Jonathan Heyden s. Ebenezer	January 25
770	Moſes Bayley S. Jonathan	
771	Mehetabel Kilborn D George	Feb. 8

772	Joſeph Chaplin S. Jeremiah	
773	Sarah Archer D. Benjamin	Feb. 15
774	Mary Nelſon D. Joſeph	
775	Mark Prime S. Mark	March 1
776	Jacob Barker S. Jacob	
	1713	
777	Eliſabeth Hobſon D. Humphery	March 29
778	Jane Jewett D. Nathanael	April 5
779	Amos Dreſſer S. Joſeph	May 10
780	Jacob Davis S. Moſes	May 17
781	Thomas Palmer S. Samuel	Jun 28
782	Sarah Bointon D Samuel	July 11
783	Thomas Johnſon s. Samuel	
784	Abraham Jewet S. Abraham	July 26
785	Eliſabeth Smith D. Benjamin	
786	Jeremiah Hibirt S. George	Augᵗ 16
787	Abigail Bridges D. John	Augᵗ 23
788	Sarah Geage D. William	
789	Sarah Barker D. James	Septʳ 13
790	Rebecca Hopkinſon D. Jeremiah	
791	Eliſabeth Nelſon D. Ephraim	Janʳʸ 31
	1714	
792	Jonathan Rogers ſ. Robert	
793	Jonathan Pierſon ſ. Stephen	March

794	John Pilsbury f. Amos	
795	Johanna Bointon D. Hilkiah	April 18
796	Hilkiah Bointon f. Hilkiah	Gemini
797	Priscilla Bointon D. Hilkiah	
798	Rebecca Pengry D. Aaron junr	April 25
799	Mehetabel Geage D. Thomas	May 16
800	Benjamin Donnell S. Nathanll	
801	John Bointon S. Jno	May 30
802	Hannah Todd D. James	
803	Mofes Forster S. Ebenezr	
804	Jofeph Scott S. Jofeph	Jun 6
805	Elifabeth Tenny D. Samll	
806	Sarah Elfworth D. Jeremiah	
807	David Chaplin S. Jeremiah	
808	David Jewet f. Stephen	
809	David Bennet f. William	Jun 13
900	Mary Bennet f. William	
901	William Bennet f. William	
902	Mercy Sawyer D. Ezekiel	July 8
903	Nathan Broclebank S. Jofeph	
904	Eliphelet Wood f. Ebenr	Augst 15
905	David Jewett S. Jofeph	Sept 5
906	Mofes Dow f. Jno	
907	Benjamin Dresser f. Samll	
908	Rebecca Smith D. John	Octob 17
909	Mary Clark D. Ebenezr	

910	Elifabeth Bointon D. Jofeph	Nov. 7
911	Sarah Palmr D. Thomas	Nov. 14
912	Jemima Jewet D. Nehemiah	Novr 21
913	Jane Palmr D. Jno	Decembr 26
914	Benjamin Archer f. Benjam.	Janry 16

1715

915	Samll Nelfon f. Jofeph	April 10
916	John Hodgkins f. Jno	April 24
917	Thomas Barkr f. Jacob	May 22
918	Jonathan Hamond f. Nathll	
919	John Bennet f. Jno	[May 29]
920	Mary Chaplin D. Jofeph	Jun 5
921	Nathll Mighill f. Nathll	Jun 12
922	John Bridges f. Jno	
923	Mary Sawyer D. John	July 10
924	Jerufha Bointon D. Ebenezr	
925	Bithiah Jewet D. Aquila	July 17
926	Nathan Plats f. Mofes	July 24
927	Mary Bayley D. Jonathan	July 31
928	William Geage f. William	Augst 14
929	Mofes Prime f. Mark	
930	Hannah Kilborn D. Georg	Augst 28
931	Rebecca Hybirt D. Georg	
932	Jane Pickard D. Francis	Septr 4
933	Mofes Jewet f. Jonath.	Septr 18
		Novr 6

934	Sarah Prime D. Samˡˡ	Feb. 5
935	Mary Woodberry D. Samˡˡ	
936	Ruth Jewet D. Joſhua	
937	Mary Kilborn Dʳ Joſeph	
938	Nathan Lambert S. Thomas	Feb. 12
939	Eliſabeth Barker D. James	
940	Mercy Smith Dʳ Benjamin	
941	Hannah Scot D. Joſeph	ffeb. 19
942	Nathan Dreiſer f. Jonath.	ffeb 26
943	Hannah Brinton D. Jnº	March 4

1716

944	Johannah Jewet D. Nathanˡˡ	March 11
945	Moſes Peirſon f. Stephen	March 18
946	Tho Elſworth f. Jeremiah	
947	Deborah Searls D. John	April 1
948	Abigail Scot D. Benjamin	April 8
949	Spencer Bennet S. William	April 14
950	Aphia Nelſon D. Ephraim	
951	Samuel Nelſon S. Joſeph	April 22
952	James Davis f. Moses	
953	Edw: Heyden S. Ebenʳ	April 29
954	Mary Palmʳ D. Samˡˡ	
955	Mercy Hopkinſon Dʳ Jeremiah	May —
956	Hannah Hāmond Dʳ Tho. Senʳ	July —.
957	Jnº Saddler f. Jnº	
960	Amos Pilſberry f. Amos	Augˢᵗ 26

961	Jnº Scott f. John	Septʳ 2
962	Samˡˡ Stickney f. Samˡ	
963	John Bennet f. Jnº	Sept. 16
964	James Dickinſon S. Georg	Septʳ 23
965	Solomon Jewet S. Stephen	
966	Nehemiah Nelſon f. Gerſhoᵐ	Octobʳ 17
967	Samˡˡ Hodgkins f. Jnº	Novʳ 25
968	Thomas Thurſton f. Danˡˡ	Decemb. 9th
969	Jonathan Pickard f. Jonathan	
970	Eliſabeth Dreiſer D. Joſeph	Decemʳ 16
971	Mary Rogers D. John	Janʳ 13
972	Joſeph Chaplin f. Jerem.	Janʳ 27
973	Nathˡˡ Hammon f. Nathˡˡ	

1717

974	John Todd f. Jnº	March 3
975	Mary Birtby D. Jer.	March 24
976	Mary Pengry D. Aaron	April 7
977	Joſeph Barker S. Jacob	April 14
978	Abel Jewet S. Aquila	
979	Jnº Chaplin f. Jnº	May 12
980	Hannah Dreiſer D. Samˡˡ	May 26
981	Edward Woodberry f. Samˡˡ	Jun 2
982	Mary Palmer D. Jnºhn	
983	Samuel Bridges f. Jnº	Jun 23
984	Edw: Sanders Adult	July 14

985	Edw. Saunders f. Edw:	July 28
986	Zacharias f. Eleonr Bointon	July 28
987	Dorothy Pickard D. Francis	Augst 11
988	Mercy Geage	gemini
	Dr Tho Geage	Augst 18
989	Elisabeth Geage	Augst 25
990	Sarah Wood D. Thomas	Septr 15
991	Solomon Smith s. John	Septr 22
992	James Davis S. Mofes	Septr 29
993	Priscilla Mighel D. Nathll	octobr 13
994	Sarah Dole D. Richard	octobr 13
995	Ebenezer Clark f. Richard	Octobr 20
996	Isaac Kilborn s. Jacob	Octobr 20
997	Abigail Nelson D. Thomas junr	Novr 10
998	Judith Piliberry D. Amos	Novr 24
999	Joseph Bointon f. hilkiah	Decemr 8
1000	Johannah Kilborn D. Joseph	Decemr 8
1001	Mary Hybirt D. George	Jany 5
1002	Ruth Clark D. Judah	Jany 12
1003	Hannah Elfworth D. Jerem.	Jan. 19

1718

1004	Mehetabel Sawyer	March 9th
	Dr Ezekll Gemini	
1005	Jane Sawyer	March 9th
1006	Benjamin Smith S. Benjam.	March 9th
1007	Ann Kilborn D. George	March 9th
1008	Elisabeth Geage Dr William	March 16
1009	Mark Prime f. Samll born after his death	March 23
1010	Amos Peirfon S. Stephen	March 23
1011	Thomas Saunders S. Edward	April 6
1012	Jeremiah Bennet S. William	April 6
1013	Elisabeth Scot D. Samuel	April 13
1014	Mary Jewett D. Nathanael	April 20
1015	Ezekiel Bayly S. Jonathan	April 27
1016	Joseph Searls f. John	May 11
1017	Daniel Barker f. James	May 11
1018	Priscilla Jewett D. Nehemiah	May 18
1019	John Choat S. Robert	May 18
1020	Mercy Hopkinson D. Jeremiah	Jun 3
1021	Hannah Palmer D. Francis	Jun 3
1022	Humphery Hobson S. Humphery	Jun 8
1023	James Heyden S. Ebenezar	Jun 29
1024	James Jewett S. Jonathan	Jun 29
1025	Jonathan Lambert f. Thomas	Jun 29
1026	David Nelson S. Joseph	July 13
1027	Joseph Saddler S. John	July 27
1028	Jonathan Smith S. John	Augst 24
1029	John Pickard S. Francis	Octob. 26
1030	Sarah Bayley D. Nathanll	Novr 23
1031	Mary Clark D. Jonathan	Nov. 30

1032	John Bointon S. John, deceafed before its birth	Decembr 28
1033	Sarah Bointon Dr Hilkiah	Janry 4th
1034	Samuel Pengry s. Job	Decembr [January] 11
1035	Mofes Pickard S. Mofes	
1036	Elifabeth Sawyer D. John	
1037	Jofhua Jewett S. Jofhua, born wthout natll paffage by ye fundamt	28 10th
1038	Rebecca Jewet D. Stephen	ffebr 1
1039	Stephen Dole f. Richard	ffebruary 8
1040	Nathanael Barker S. Jacob	ffebr 15
	1719	
1041	Ann Pengry D. Aaron	March 15
1042	John Drefser S. Samuel	
1043	Daniel Chaplin S. Jeremiah	April 5
1044	Sarah Stickny Dr Samuel	
1045	Sarah Thurston Dr Daniel	May 17
1046	Martha Scott D Jofeph	Jun 7
1047	Rebecca Hodgkins Dr John	Jun 21
1048	Jofeph Kilborn S. Jofeph	July 5
1049	Amos Jewett S. Aquila	
1050	Jofeph Birtby S. Jeremiah	July 26
1051	Phœbe Kilborn Dr George	Augst 9
1052	Mary Prime D. Mark	Augst 16
1053	Samuel Tenny s. Samuel	Augst 23
1054	John Pickard S. Jonathan	
1055	Elifabeth Saunders Dr Edward	Septr 28
1056	Brattlebank Todd S. Samuel	
1057	Mary Hammon D. Thomas	Octobr 11
1058	John Duty S. Samuel	Octobr 18
1059	Thomas Hammon S. Nathanael	
1060	Ruth Scott D. Samuel	Novr 1
1061	Jonathan Platts S. Mofes	Novr 15
1062	Thomas Birtbe S. Thomas	Novr 29
1063	Lydia Scott D. Benjamin junr	Decembr 6
1064	Jeremiah Ellworth s. Jeremiah	
1065	Hannah Palmer D. John	Janry 3
1066	Hannah Mighill D Nathanll	Janry 10
1067	Jofeph Rogers S. John	Janry 17
1068	Edna Pickard D. Francis	Janry 24
1069	Samuel Wood S. Thomas	ffebry 7
1070	Ruth Todd D. John junr	ffeb. 14
1071	Joshua Jewett S. Jofhua	
1072	Mary Palmer D. Thomas	ffebry 21
	1720	
1073	James Nevins S. Martha, a Scotch woman,	April 10
1074	Mary Jarvis D. James	April 10
1075	Mary Peirfon D. Stephen	May 8
1076	Abigail Nelfon D. Gerfhom	May 22

1077	Jonathan Barker S. James	May 29
1078	Elifabeth Bennet D. John	
1079	Mary Nelfon D. Ephraim	June 26
1080	Ebenezar Chaplin S. Jeremiah	July 8
1081	Mofes Bennet S. David	
1082	Benjamin Sawer s. Ezek[ll]	July 23
1083	Mofes Pilbury s. Amos	Aug[st] 7
1084	Sarah Jewett D. Jonathan	Aug[st] 21
1085	David Hammon S. David	
1086	Nehemiah Hopkinfon S. Jeremiah	Sept. 11
1087	Stephen Palmer S. Francis	
1088	Jacob Smith S. Benjam̄	Sept[r] 18
1089	Mofes Pengry s. Job	Nov[r] 13
1090	Peter Woodberry f. Samuel	Decemb[r] 11
1091	Hannah Davis D. Mofes	Decemb[r] 18
1092	Nathanael Jewet s. Nathan[ll]	decemb[r] 25
1093	Abiel Sadler S. John	
1094	Johannah Pickard D. Jonathan	Jan[ry] 22
1095	Mary Barker D. Jacob	Jan[ry] 29
1096	Ebenezer Kilborn f. Jofeph	Feb[ry] 12
	1721	
1097	Mary Kilborn D[r] George	March 26
1098	Sarah Jarvis D[r] James	May
1099	Martha Pengry D[r] Aaron	
1100	Ruth Bointon D[r] Hilkiah	July 2
1101	Thoms Tenny S[n] Sam[ll]	July 9
1102	Samuel Geage S[n] Thomas	Septemb[r] 10
1103	James Platts S[n] James	Sept[r] 24
1104	Lucy Lambert D[r] Thomas	October 1
1105	John Crosby S[n] Jonathan	Octob[r] 8
1106	Jane Rogers D[r] Robert	Octob[r] 15
1107	Ann Chaplin D[r] Jeremiah	
1108	Abigail Rowfe D[r] William	Octob[r] 29
1109	Jonathan Shepard Adult	
1110	Thomas Saunders S[n] Edward	Nov[r] 5
1111	David Pickard S[n] Mofes	Nov[r] 12
1112	Caleb Jewet S[n] Nehemiah	Nov[r] 19
1113	Mehetabel Pickard D[r] Francis	Novemb[r] 26
1114	Sarah Northen D[r] John	
1115	Mofes Chaplin S[n] John	
1116	Samuel Jewet s[n] Jofhua	Jan[ry] 21
1117	Hannah Scott D[r] Samuel	
1118	Daniel Todd s[n] John	
1119	Jonathan Elfworth s[n] Jeremiah	January 28
1120	Jeremiah Clark s[n] Judah	
1121	Jofeph Hammon s[n] Nathan[ll]	Feb[ry] 4
1122	Jane Pfilberry D[r] Amos Pilfbury	Feb[ry] 11
1123	Sarah Palmer D[r] John Palmer	

No.	Name	Date
1146	Jane Pengry Dʳ Job	} Octob. 7
1147	Hephziba Birtby Dʳ Ebenezʳ	
1148	Sarah Payſon Dʳ Samuel	Novʳ 25
1149	Mark Platts son James	Decemb. 16
1150	Mary Creaſie Dʳ Jonathan	Janʳʸ 13
1151	Mercy Geage Dʳ William	
1152	Moſes Plummer Sⁿ Aaron	} ffeb. 17
	1723	
1153	Jeremiah Jewet sⁿ Aquila	
1154	Aaron Clark sⁿ Jonathan	} March 3
1155	Eliſabeth Kilborn Dʳ Jacob	
1156	Stephen Peirſon son Stephen	
1157	Jane Bointon Dʳ Hilkiah	March 10
1158	Eliſabeth Chaplin Dʳ Jeremiah	March 17
1159	George Hybirt Sⁿ George	March 24
1160	Jane Kilborn Dʳ George	March 31
1161	Faith Jewet Dʳ Nathanᵘ	April 21
1162	Jane Pickard Dʳ Francis	Jun 23
1163	Jane Saunders Dʳ Edward	Jun 30
1164	Mary Jewet Dʳ Joſeph	July 14
1165	Mary Tod Dʳ John junʳ	Sep. 8
1166	Moſes Stickney sⁿ Samuel	
1167	Ann Tenny Dʳ Samuel	Octobʳ 13
1168	Hannah Goodwin Adult	
1169	Mary Birtby Dʳ Thomas	} Octobʳ 20
1170	Jeremiah Birtby sⁿ Jonathan	

No.	Name	Date
1124	Jeremiah Birtby sⁿ Jeremiah	} Febʳʸ 11
1125	Sarah Duty Dʳ Samuel Duty	
1126	Mehetabel Hobſon Dʳ Humph- ery	
1127	Jonathan Wood sⁿ Thomas	} Febʳʸ 25
	1722	
1128	Thomas Palmer Sⁿ Thomas	March 4
1129	Jonathan Palmer Sⁿ Samuel	
1130	Mary Brown	} Children of } March 11
1131	James Brown	} JamesBrown
1132	John Brown	
1133	Suſanna Scott D. Joſeph	April 1
1134	Thomas Mighel sⁿ Nathanael	
1135	Lucy Heyden Dʳ Ebenezʳ	} April 8
1136	Eliſabeth Creaſie Dʳ John	
1137	Daniel Bridges S. John	April 29
1138	Mary Barker Dʳ Jacob	May 27
1139	Phillips Bennet sⁿ David	July 29
1140	Jeremiah Hopkinſon sⁿ Jere- miah	} Augᵗ 12
1141	Mary Davis Dʳ Moſes	
1142	Abigail Bradſtreet Dʳ Moſes Junʳ	Augᵗ 15
1143	Francis Nelſon Sⁿ Samuel	Septʳ 2
1144	John Sawer Sⁿ John	} September 30
1145	Hannah Woodberry Dʳ Samuel	

No.	Name	Date
1171	Elifabeth Pickard Dr Mofes	Octobr 27
1172	John Pilfberry Sn Amos	Sept 17
1173	Elifabeth Dickinfon Dr Jno	Decemr 1
1174	Jemima Bennet Dr William	Janᵞ 5
1175	Stephen Palmer sr Timothy	Janᵞ 12
1176	Lydia Jewet Dr Samuel	Febᵞ 23

1724

No.	Name	Date
1176	Samuel Kelly sn Samll	March 1
1177	Samuel Payfon Sn Samll	March 15
1178	Elifabeth Payfon Dr Eliot	March 29
1179	Sarah Pengry Dr Aaron	April 5
1180	Nathanael Ellworth sn Jeremiah	
1181	Sarah Palmer Dr John	} April 19
1182	Jane Northend Dr John	
1183	Sarah Bridges	
	Drˢ John, Gemini	} May 31
1184	Ruth Bridges	
1185	Jeremiah Mighel Sn Nathanael	Jun 14
1186	Sarah Peirfon Dr Stephen	Jun 21
1187	Thomas Dickinfon Sn Thomas junr	} July 11
1188	Jonathan Bayly sr John	Augˢt 2
1889	Sufannah Scott Dr Samll	
	Gemini	} Augˢt 16
1190	Jane Scott Dr Samll	

No.	Name	Date
1191	Samuel Duty son Samuel	Sept 13
1192	Jeremiah Birtby sn Ebenezr	Sept 27
1193	Ann Creafle Dr John	Novr 1
1194	Joseph Smith sn Benjamin	
1195	Humphery Woodberry sn Nathan	} Novr 22
1196	Martha Killborn Dr Georg	Decembr 13
1197	Jeremiah Chaplin sn Jeremiah	January 3
1198	Francis Pickard sn Francis	} Febᵞ 7
1199	James Drefser sn John junr	

1725

No.	Name	Date
1200	Elifabeth Plummer Dr Aaron	March 7
1201	Philips Payfon sn Samuel	April 11
1202	Mehetable Rowfe Dr Abigail	Aprill 23
1203	Jane Pickard Dr Jonathan	May 2
1204	Joseph Saunders sn Edward	May 9
1205	Isaac Birtby son Jonathan	} July 11
1206	Elifabeth Todd Dr John	
1207	Margaret Wood Dr Thomas	July 18
1208	Mary Bradstreet Dr Mofes junr	July 25
1209	Amos Dole sn Richard	} Augˢt 1
1210	John Kelley sn Samuel	
1211	Hilkiah Bointon sn hilkiah	Gemini
1212	Mehetable Bointon Dr hilkiah	} Augˢt 8
1213	Samuel Jewet sn Jofhua	

No.	Name	Date
1214	Jedidiah Killborn sn Jedidiah	} Augst 15
1215	Elisabeth Bayly Dr John	
1216	William Dow sn Jeremiah	Septembr 5
1217	Hannah Dickinson Dr Thomas	Septr 19
1218	Moses Jewet son Samll	} Octobr 10
1219	Ann Jewet Dr Aquila	
1220	Joseph Platts sn Abel junr	} Febry 20
1221	Isaac Foster sn Danll	} Febry

1726

No.	Name	Date
1222	John Wheeler	} March 6
1223	Elisabeth Wheeler	
1224	Elisabeth Palmer Dr Francis	April 3
1225	Edward Payson sn Edward	} April 10
1226	Joseph Bridges sn John	
1227	John Pengry sn Job	April 24
1228	Nathanll Geage sn William	May 8
1229	Elisabeth Bayly Dr Joseph	May 15
1230	Samuel Deuty son Samll	May 22
1231	Sarah Dickinson Dr John	Jun 5
1232	Margaret Elsworth Dr Jeremiah	Jun 19
1233	Sarah Tenny Dr Samll	Jun 26
1234	Jane Scott Dr Benjamin	} July 10
1235	Sarah Birtbe Dr Ebenezer	
1236	John Hodgkin sn John	} July 24
1237	John Pickard sn Moses	

No.	Name	Date
1238	Samuel Scott son Samll	Augst 14
1239	William Stickny son Samuel	Augst 28
1240	Joshua Todd son John	} Septembr 18
1241	Moses Dresr sn Jno junr	
1242	Elisabeth Mighel Dr Nathanll	Octobr 2
1243	Stephen Peirson sn Stephen	
1244	Thomas Hybirt sn George	} Octobr 30
1245	Francis Johnson sn Daniel	
1246	Mercy Platts Dr James	Novembr 13
1247	Mary Jewet Dr Benjamin	Novembr 27
1248	Elisabeth Kelly Dr Samuel	Decembr 25
1249	John Bagley his Dr Elisabeth	Jany 5
1250	Susanna Hobson Dr Moses	Jany 22
1251	Moses Woodberry sn Nathan	March 5

1727

No.	Name	Date
1252	Samuel Northen sn John	March 12
1253	Mary Smith Dr Benjamin	} March 19
1254	Mehetabel Palmer Dr John	
1255	Nathanael Bayly sn Joseph	
1256	Mary Saunders Dr Edward	March 26
1257	Stephen Northen sn Ezekll	April 23
1258	Thomas Nelson sn Samuel	April 30
1259	David Abbot Topsfield &c.	
1260	Priscilla Jewet Dr Stephen	} July 2
1261	Mary Creasie Dr Samuell	

No.	Name	Date
1262	Daniel Dow son Jeremiah	} July 23
1263	Dorcas Pengry Dr Aaron	
1264	Mercy Forfter Dr Daniel	Augst 20
1265	Simon Stickny s. John	Novembr 12
1266	Mofes Clark sn Jonathan	Decembr 3d
1266	Stephen Jewet sn Aquilla	} Decembr 31
1267	Edward —— Adult	
1268	Edward Payfon son Eliot	Jany 14
1269	Mofes Bradftreet son Nathan	} ffeby 4
1270	Mary Platts Dr Abell	
1271	James Platts son James	Feby 11th
1272	Mary Payfon Dr Samuell	} Feby 18
1273	John Dickinfon son John	
1274	John Johnfon son John	Feby 25
1275	Hannah Creatie Dr Abell	March 10
	1728	
1276	Joseph Killborn sn Jacob	March 17
1277	Mary Davis Dr Nathan	} April 7
1278	Isreal Davis sn Nathan	
1279	Eliphalet Payfon sn Eliphalet	} May 5
1280	Mary Hammon Dr David	
1281	Mofes Woodberry sn Hanna	May 12
1282	Lydia Pickard Dr Mofes	May 28
1283	William Price sn William	} Jun 3
1284	John Palmer sn Timothy	
1285	Hannah Northen Dr Ezekll junr	Augst 4
1286	Francis Pengry son Job	Augst 11
1287	Hanna Dickinfon Dr Tho junr	Septr 29
1288	Mary Geage Dr William	} Octobr 6
1289	Lucy Pickard Dr Jonathan	
1290	Humphery Saunders sr Edward	
	ward	
1291	Jemima Bifhop Dr Jofiah	} Octobr 13
1292	Thomas Jewet sn Jofhua	
1293	Sarah Palmer Dr Francis	Octobr 27
1294	Samuel Hobfon sn Humphery	Decembr 1
1295	John Hobfon son Mofes	Decembr 8
1296	Thomas Todd son John junr	} Decembr 15
1297	Edward Payfon sn Edward	
1298	John Bayly sn David	Jany 5
1299	John Chapman sn Edward	} Jany 19
1300	Pricilla Birtby Dr Ebenezar	
1301	Abigail Davis Dr Nathan	} Jany 26
1302	Mofes Tenny son Samuel	
1303	Jane Todd Dr John senr	Feby 2
1304	Elifabeth Payfon Dr David ibid	feby 2
1305	Richard Esty sn Richard	Feby 9
1306	Nathanll Elfworth sn Jeremiah	Feb. 23
	1729	
1307	Mary Creafie Dr John	} March 16
1308	Sarah Jackfon Dr Jofhua	
1309	Mary Harris Dr John	

No.	Name	Date
1310	Mary Jewet Dr Nathaniel	March 23
1311	Elisabeth Stickny Dr Samuel	March 23
1312	Samson Killborn sn Jedidiah	March 23
1313	Mary Nelson Dr Ephraim	March 30
1314	Gibbins Jewet sn Joseph	Aprill 13
1315	Jeremiah Peirson sn Stephen	Aprill 13
1316	Elisabeth Chaplin Dr Jeremiah	Aprill 20
1317	Mehetabel Creasie Dr Abell	Aprill 20
1318	Joseph Pickard sn Joseph	May 18
1319	Hannah Smith Dr Benjamin	June 1
1320	Jeremiah Dow sn Jeremiah	Jun 22
1321	Daniel Bayly sn Joseph	Jun 29
1322	John Bradstreet sn Nathanll	July 13
1323	Sarah Rowie Dr Abigail	July 13
	1730	
1324	Dan Foster sn Daniel	Augt 21
1325	Jeremiah Hybirt sn George	Septr 28
1326	Ruth Plats Dr Abell	October 5
1327	John Palmer son John	Novembr 3
1328	Jedidia Bayly son John	Nov. 9
1329	Hannah Platts Dr James	Novemb. 16
1330	Judah Johnson sn Danll	Febry 22
1331	Elisabeth Stickny Dr John	Febry 22
1332	Daniel Stickny sn Samuel	Aprill 12
1333	Hannah Cooper Dr Moses	April 12
1334	Elisabeth Jewet Dr John jun	May 3
1335	Mary Woodberry Dr Nathan	Jun 28
1336	Lidia Pickard Dr Moses	July 12
1337	Sewall Northern s. Ezekiel	Augst 30
1338	John Harris sn John	Octobr 11
1339	Dorothy Pickard Dr Francis	Octobr 11
1340	Lydia Davis Dr Nathan	Novembr 8
1341	Joseph Peirson sn John	Novembr 29
1342	Joshua Pickard sn Jonathan	Decembr 20
1343	Jane Payson Dr Eliphalet	Jany 17
1344	Ebenezar Birtbe sn Ebenezer	Febry 14
1345	Sarah Dreiser Dr John junr	Febry 14
1346	Elisabeth Jackson Dr Caleb	Febry 14
	1731	
1347	John Creasie sn John	Aprill 11
1348	Jacob Bayly son David	Aprill 18
1349	Nathan Birtby sn Samuel	Aprill 18
1350	Jane Nelson Dr Solomon	June 6
1351	James Payson son Eliot	June 27
1352	Samuel Hobson s. Moses	July 11
1353	Rebecca Peirson Dr Stephen	Augst 29
1354	Ebenezer Todd sn John junll	Augst 29
1355	Hannah Foster Dr Danll	Septembr 26
1356	Phinehas Hammon sn David	Septr 7
1357	Edna Dreiser Dr ——	Septr 7
1358	Joseph Dole sn Enoch	Decembr 12
1359	Benjamin Sawyer sn Ezekll	Jany 2

1732

1360	Judith Plats Dr James	} Jany 16
1361	James Creaie sn Abell	
1362	Samuel Davis sn Nathan	} Feby 27
1363	Dummer Jewet sn Jedidiah	
1364	Ann Hobson Dr Jeremiah	} April 30

1365	Hanna Jewet Dr George	May 14
1240	Asa Pengry s. Job	May 28

[Recorded by the Revd Jedediah Jewet *fifth* minister.]

EARLY RECORDS OF ROWLEY, MASS.

(Concluded from Vol. xxxv, p. 256.)

BY GEORGE B. BLODGETTE.

An account of ye Perfons Baptized by me since my ordination. [Recorded by the Revd Jedediah Jewet.]

1729

1	William Todd Son of Daniel	Dec. 14

1730

2	William Hobson Sn of Jeremy	Mar. 29
3	Juda Cresey datr of David	Apr. 26
4	Sarah Price datr of William	May 24
5	Sarah Chapman dtr of Edward	June 21
6	Hannah Johnson dtr of John	July 5
7	Zebulon Eastick Son of Richard	} July 5
8	Edna Jewet dtr of George	July 19
9	Lydia Bishop dtr of Josiah	} Aug. 23
10	Moses Cooper Sn of Moses	
11	William Cresey son of Abel	Sep. 13
12	Abigail Kilborn datr of George	Oct. 18
13	Hannah Bradstreet dtr of Nathall	Nov. 9
14	Lydia Sanders dtr of Edward	Dec. 13

4 males & 9 Females this Year

1731

15	William Dickinson son of John	Feb. 7.
16	David Burpee son of Jonathan	Mar. 28
17	Elisabeth Payson dtr of Samll	} May 29
18	Mehetabel Dresser dtr of Daniel	
19	Sarah Lancaster dtr of Thomas	June 20
20	Sarah Tenny dtr of Samll	Aug. 1
21	Patience Palmer dtr of Timothy	Aug. 8
22	Susanna Cresey dtr of Samll	Aug. 15
23	Nathan Frazer son of Nathan	Aug. 26
24	Thomas Sparks son of John	} Sep. 12
25	Amos Bayley Sn of Joseph	
26	Mary Jewet dtr of Joshua	Oct. 3
27	Joram Johnson son of Daniel	Oct. 17
28	Samll Pickard son of Joseph	Nov. 9.
29	Hannah Bradstreet dtr of Nathall	Nov. 14
30	Priscilla Downing dtr of Jona- than	} Dec. 26

7 males & 9 Females this year

1732

31	Hephzibah Dow dr Jeremy	Jan. 9.
32	Francis Palmer Son of Francis	} Jan. 23
33	Moses Northend son of Samll	
34	Peter Cooper son of Leonard	Mar. 5
35	James Todd son of Jonathan	May 7.
36	Elisabeth Kilborn dr of Jedidiah	May 21
37	Priscilla Cooper dr of Moses	June 18
	Joshua Dickinson son of Thomas	
38	William Dickinson son of John	} July 30
39	Hannah Burpee dr of Samll	
40	Hannah Pickard dr of Moses	Aug. 6
41	Sarah Chaplin dr of Jonathan	
42	Daniel Hobson son of Moses	Sep. 3
43	Edward Northend son of Ezekiel	
44	Hannah Hodgskin dr of John	Oct. 1
45	Bristo Mr Paysons negroe Servant Adult.	} Nov. 5
46	Nathan Frazer son of Nathan	Nov. 26
47	Nehemiah Johnson son of John	Dec. 10
48	Daniel Woodberry son of Nathan	Dec. 31
	11 males & 7 Females this year	

1733

49	Hannah Harris dr of John	Jan. 7.
50	Benjamin Bishop son of Josiah	} Feb. 18
51	Jane Palmer dr of Timothy	
52	Elisabeth Stickney dr of Samll	} Apr. 8
53	Samll Lancaster Son of Thomas	
54	Samll Hidden son of Eben	Apr. 15
55	Mary Chapman dr of Edward	May 6
56	Priscilla Jewet dr of Aquila	May 27
57	Sarah Hibbert dr of James	June 3
58	Hannah Payson dr of Samll	June 10
59	Samuel Pickard son of Joseph	July 8
60	Elisabeth Dresser dr of John junr	} July 22
61	Elisabeth Lambert dr of Thomas junr	} Aug. 12
62	Sarah Bayley dr of David	
63	Susanna Cresey dr of Samll	} August 19
64	Mary Dresser dr of Daniel	
65	William Sanders son of Edward	} Aug. 26
66	Sarah Pearson dr of John	
67	Elisabeth Boynton dr of Ephraim	
68	Sarah Martin dr of Daniel	Sep. 2
69	Obadiah Johnson Son of Daniel	Oct. 14
70	Sarah Cresey dr of Abel	Nov. 18
71	Eliot Payson ye son of Eliot	Dec. 9.

72	Ryal } My black Servant	Dec. 23
73	and Titus } children	
	9 males & 16 Females this year	

1734

74	Jonathan Downing Son of Jonathan	Jan. 13
75	Phebe Payson dr of Edward ℣ Mr Chandler	Jan. 20
76	Mark Cresey son of John	Jun 27
77	Elisabeth Foster dr of Daniel	Mar. 3
78	John Sawyer son of Ezekiel	March 24
79	Sarah Plats dr of James	April 21
80	John Northend son of Saml	
81	Moses Hobson son of Moses	June 2
82	Elisabeth Northend dr of Ezekiel	June 9.
83	Paul Jewet my son	June 16
84	Ruth Palmer dr of Francis	June 30
85	Joseph Hobson son of Jeremiah	July 7
86	Joseph Chapman son of Edward	July 14
87	Elisabeth Dickinson dr of Thomas jur	Aug. 4.
88	John Jewet son of John jur	Aug. 11
89	Saml Prime son of Joshua	Aug. 18
90	Nathanael Bradstreet son of Nathal	Sep. 1.
91	Mary Jewet dr of Edward	Sep. 15
92	Lydia Sanders dr of Edward	Sep. 29.
93	Samuel Burpee son of Saml	
94	Jeremiah Dickinson son of George	Oct. 6.
95	Sarah Cooper dr of Leonard	Nov. 24
96	Sarah Pickard dr of Francis	Dec. 22.
97	Ephraim Hidden son of Eben	
	14 Males & 10 Females this year	

1735

98	David Bayley son of David	Feb. 16
99	Solomon Frazer son of Nathan	Feb. 23
100	Eunice Cresey dr of Abel	March 9
101	Ephraim Boynton son of Ephraim	March 16
102	Amos Pickard son of Moses	March 30
103	Phoebe Harris dr of John	
104	Mary Martin dr of Daniel	
105	Jedidiah Barker son of James	April 20
106	Sarah Jewet dr of Eliphalet	
107	Jonathan Todd son of Jonathan	April 27
108	Ezekiel Hodgskin son of John	May 4
109	Paul Lancaster son of Thomas	May 25
110	Abel Plats son of Abel	
111	Mary Johnson dr of Jonathan	June 1

112 Isreal Woodberry son of Nathan June 8
113 Jacob Pickard son of Joseph June 29
114 Sarah Dresser dr of Samuel junr July 20
115 Moses Johnson son of John Aug. 10
116 Alijah Johnson son of Jonathan Sep. 7.
117 Sarah Lambert datr of Thomas junr } Sep. 21
118 Isaiah Johnson son of Daniel Oct. 19
119 Ezekiel Bradstreet son of Nathall Oct. 25
120 Jane Dickinson datr of Thomas junr } Nov. 16.
121 Isaac Davis son of Nathan Nov. 30
122 Jemima Bishop datr of Josiah Dec. 28
122 Moses Hobson son of Moses } Dec. 14
123 Joshua Prime son of Joshua

18 Males & 9 Females ye last year

1736

124 Elisabeth Hobson dr of Jeremiah Jan. 4.
125 Sarah Todd dr of John junr } Jan. 11.
126 Samuel Cresey Sn of Samll Jan. 18
127 Mary Payson datr of Eliot } Feb. 1.
128 Elisabeth Northend datr of Ezekiel
129 John Jewet Son of John Feb. 15
130 Olive Prime datr of Mark Feb. 22
131 Lucey Cresey datr. of John Mar. 7

132 John Chapman son of Edward Mar. 21
133 Richard Pearson son of John Apr. 11.
134 Jonathan Todd son of Jonathan Apr. 18
135 Rebekah Plats datr of James junr } Apr. 25.
136 Moses Kœsar son of Moses May 9.
137 Dorothy Jewet my own Babe July 18.
138 William Martin son of Daniel Aug. 1.
139 Anne Sawyer datr. of Ezekiel
140 Jemima Dresser datr of John junr } Aug. 22.
141 Dorothy Northend datr of Samll
142 Priscilla Jewet datr of Eliphalet
143 Caleb Cresey Son of Abel Sep. 5
144 Anne Lowel datr of Richard Sep. 12
145 John Boynton son of Ephraim Sep. 19
146 Martha Robbens datr of William Sep. 19
147 David Stickney } Gemini sons of } Sep. 26
148 Jonathan Stickney } Samll
149 John Sanders son of Edward Oct 31.
150 John Cresey son of David Oct. 31
151 London Mrs Paysons Negro womans Child Dec. 12
152 Price Hidden son of Eben

153	Lucey Jewet da^{tr} of George	Dec. 19
154	Jeremiah Dickinson son of George	Dec. 26
	16 Males & 15 Females	

1737

155	Susanna Hibbert da^{tr} of James	Jan. 9
156	Moses Wood son of Thomas jun^r	
157	Moses Jewet son of Mark	Jan. 30
158	Moses Hopkinson son of Moses	Feb. 6.
159	Elizabeth Todd da^{tr} of John	May 8
160	Jane Payson da^{tr} of Eliphalet	May 22
161	Eliot Payson son of Eliot	
162	Mary Northend da^{tr} of Ezekiel	May 29
163	James Plats son of James	July 24
164	Thomas Barker son of Jacob	
165	Nathanael Bradstreet Son of Nath^{ll}	
166	Symond Chapman son of Edward	July 31
167	Sarah Prime da^{tr} of Joshua	
168	Mark Frazer son of Nathan	
169	Benjamin Dresser of Sam^{ll} jun^r	Aug. 14
170	Sarah Martin da^{tr} of Daniel	Aug. 21

171	Sam^{ll} Palmer son of Timothy	Aug. 28
172	Timothy Harris son of John	
173	Nehemiah Johnson son of John	Sep. 11
174	Elisabeth Palmer da^{tr} of Daniel	Sep. 18
175	Joseph Pearson son of John	
176	Susanna Hobson da^{tr} of Moses	Octo. 2.
177	Sarah Barker da^{tr} of James	
178	Daniel Scot son of Joseph jun^r	Octo. 16
179	Nehemiah Jewet Son of Jeremy	Oct. 30
180	Dorothy Lancaster da^{tr} of Thomas	Nov. 6
181	Elisabeth Jewet da^{tr} of John	Nov. 20
182	Lucey Stickney da^{tr} of John	Dec. 4
183	Sarah Pickard da^{tr} of Joseph	Dec. 18
	16 Males & 13 Females	

1738

184	James Cresey son of Abel	Jan. 1.
185	Joseph Hobson Son of Jeremiah	Jan. 15
186	Bridget Pemberton Da^{tr} of John	
187	Pierce Bayley Son of David	Feb. 12
188	Mary Jewet D^r of Mark	Feb. 19
189	Asa Todd son of Jonathan	March 12
190	Eunice Hodgskin d^{tr} of John	June 4
191	Anne Sawyer D^r of Ezekiel	July

192   Mary Cresey } Twin Dau[rs] of
193   Sarah Cresey } John   Sep. 3.
194   Sarah Hibbert da[tr] of James
195   Jonathan Jewet son of Eliphalet   Sep. 24
196   Sarah Johnson d[tr] of Jonathan   Oct. 8.
197   Abel Plats Son of Abel   Oct. 15.
198   Sarah Dickinson da[tr] of
     Thomas
199   Elisabeth Johnson da[tr] of } Octo. 29
     Daniel
200   Judith Cresey da[tr] of David   Nov. 5
201   Ezekiel Sanders son of Ed-
     ward   } Nov. 19
202   Sarah Northend da[tr] of Eze-
     kiel
203   Mehetabel Lambert d[tr] of
     Thomas ju[r]   Dec. 10

7 Males 13 Females

1739

204   Moses Lowel son of Richard   Jan. 7
205   Samuel Hidden Son of Eben   Jan. 28
206   Jane Bradstreet D[r] of Nathanael   Feb. 25
207   Ruth Palmer da[tr] of Daniel   March 4
208   David Hobson Son of Moses   March 11

209   Sarah Wood dau[tr] of Thomas } May 6
     jun[r]
210   Paul Jewet son of Joshua
211   Joseph Jewet son of George } May 13
212   Daniel Dickinson son of George   June 10
213   Joanna Hammond D[r] of David   June 24
214   Sam[ll] Pearson son of John   July 1.
215   Jedidiah Cooper son of Leonard   July 15
216   Mark Dresser son of Sam[ll]   Sep. 2
217   Priscilla Johnson da[tr] of John   Sep. 16
218   Daniel Todd Son of John   Oct. 14
219   Mary Gage D[r] of Thomas   Nov. 4
220   Mary Cooper D[tr] of Samuel   Dec. 30
221   Sarah Jewet D[tr] of John
222   Eunice Jewet D[tr] of Jeremy } Jan. 13.
223   Joseph Dresser son of David
     jun[r]
224   Amos Bayley son of David   Jan. 27

12 Males 9 Females

1740

225   Jane Bayley D[r] of Sam[ll]   March 2
226   Sarah Hobson da[tr] of Jeremy
227   Katherine Jewet da[tr] of Mark } March 30
228   Francis Palmer son of Francis   May 4
229   Elisabeth Barker da[tr] of Jacob   May 25

230	Joseph Pickard son of Joseph	June 8
231	David Cresey son of David	June 15
232	Lydia Lancaster dᵗʳ of Thomas	June 29
233	Sarah Boynton dᵗʳ of Ephraim	June 1.
234	Joseph Chapman son of Edward	June 1.
235	John Osborn son of John junʳ	June 20
236	Nathanael Bradstreet son of Natˡˡ	
237	Isreal Hazzen son of Isreal	July 27
238	Elisabeth Clark Daᵗʳ of Danielˡ	
239	Moses Sawyer son of Ezekiel	Aug. 24
240	a child Daniel Martin [inter lined]	
240	Mary the Daughter of Mary Bennet	Sep. 7
241	James the son of Mary Pearson	Sep. 14
242	Mary Indus my servᵗ Adult	Nov. 2
244	Jane Pickard daᵗʳ of Jonathan	Nov. 23
245	Lydia Plats daᵗʳ of Nathan	Dec. 7
246	Eben Todd son of Jeremiah	Dec. 14
247	Sarah Brocklebank daᵗʳ of Nathan	28 Dec.

10 Males 13 Females

1741

Samˡˡ Prime son of Joshua

248	Mary Palmer dᵗʳ of Daniel	Jan. 11

249	Mary Payson dᵗʳ of Eliphalet	Jan. 18
250	Betty Lowel dᵗʳ of Richard	
251	Sarah Hidden daᵗʳ of Eben	March 8
252	William Perkins son of Zacheus	March 15
253	Moses Frazer son of Nathan	March 29
254	Francis Johnson son of Thomas	
255	Phœbe Jewet dᵗʳ of Eliphalet	Apr. 19
256	Sarah Jewet daᵗʳ of George	May 3
257	John Cresey son of John	May 10
258	Dinah Mʳ Northends Negroe	May 24
259	Nathan Todd son of Jonathan	June 7
260	James Bayley son of James	
261	Edna Plats daᵗʳ of Moses	
262	George Hibbert son of James	June 14
263	Joshua Burpee son of Joseph	
264	Elisabeth Pearson daᵗʳ of John	July 5
—	John Bayley son of Samˡˡ	July 19
265	John Bayley son of David	Sep. 13
266	Sibbey Nathˡˡ Mighills negro woman	
267	Abel Cresey son of Abel	Oct. 11
268	David Dickinson son of George	Oct 18
269	Daniel Johnson son of Jonathan	Nov. 15.
270	Devonshire Mʳ. Osborns Negro	Jan. 24
271	Susanna Johnson daᵗʳ of John	Jan. 24

272 Sam^ll Todd son of John
273 Hannah Wood da^tr of Thomas jun^r } Feb. 7

13 Males and 13 Females

1742

274 Bethiah Dresser da^tr of Sam^ll — March 21
275 Moses Scot son of Joseph — March 28
276 James Jewet son of Mark } April 4
277 Moses Plats son of Nathan
— Moses Duty son of Moses } April 11
278 Mary Dresser da^tr of David
279 Lydia Hobson D^r of Moses } May 23
280 Amos Boynton son of Ephraim
281 Paul Dickinson son of James
282 Susanna Cooper da^tr of Leonard — May 6
283 Violet & } two Negro children } June 13
284 Phillis } of Sibbys
285 Ruth Tredwels child of Jona- than Tredwels } July —
286 Amos Pickard son of Joseph — Aug. 22.
287 Sarah Clark Da^tr of Aaron
288 Elizabeth Bayley d^r of James } Sep. 19
289 Mary Barker d^r of James jun^r
290 Moses Prime s. of Joshua — Sep. 19
291 Hannah Dresser d^r of Daniel — Oct. 17

292 Daniel Kilborn son of Joseph — Oct 24
293 David Todd son of Jeremiah } Nov. 7
294 Jane Jewet da^tr of Moses
295 Thomas Bayley son of Sam^ll
296 Elisabeth Gage da^tr of Thos } Dec. 12
Thomas Lancaster son of Thomas
297 Moses-Paul Payson son of Eliot — Jan. 30
298 Jane Jewet d^r of George } Feb. 20
299 Cæsar a negroe man-servant
300 Elisabeth Brocklebank da^tr of Nathan } Feb. 27
301 Hannah Hibbert da^tr of James

13 Males and 15 Females ye Year

1743

302 Thomas Pickard son of Jona- than } March 6
303 Humphry Pickard son of Moses jun^r
304 Jacob Barker son of Jacob
305 Jonathan Lambert son Tho. — Apr. 24
Mary Jewet daughter of John — May 1
306 Susanna Johnson da^tr of John } May 8
307 John Todd son of John jun^r
308 Beriah Clark son of Daniel — May 22

309	Moses Cooper son of Leonard	May 29
310	Moses Plats son of Moses	July 24
311	James Hidden son of Eben	Aug. 14
312	Joanna Burpee Dʳ of Joseph	
313	Jane Martin Dʳ of Daniel	Aug. 21
314	Nathanael Bayley son of David	
315	Jane Woodman datʳ of Joshua	Sep. 4.
316	Elisabeth Johnson datʳ of Thomas	
317	Jane Osborn dtʳ of John	
318	Elisabeth Bradstreet Dʳ of Nathˡˡ	Sep. 25.
319	Moses Dickinson son of James	
320	Ruth-Duty Pearson Dᵗʳ of Mary Pearson	
321	Elisabeth Duty datʳ of Moses	Oct. 16
322	Isaac Smith son of Benj,	
323	David Cresey son of David	Dec. 11
324	Jedidiah Boynton son of Ephraim	Jan. 22
—	Stephen Jewet son of Eliphalet	
325	Jane Johnson Dʳ of Jonathan	Feb. 26
	14 Males 10 Females	

1744

326	Elisabeth Plats Dᵗʳ of Nathan	March 11
327	Amos Dickinson son of George	Mar. 18
328	Hannah Wood Dʳ of Thomas	Apr. 1
329	Ruth Jewet Dʳ of Mark	April 22
330	Mary Jewet Dʳ of Jeremiah	May 13
331	Edward Bishop son of Benjamin	27 May
332	Aaron Jewet son of Moses	
333	Amos Dresser son of David	June 3
334	Mary Bishop Adult	June 17
335	Joseph Kilborn son of Ebenezer	July 1
336	Susanna Lowel Dʳ of Richard	
337	Amos Stickney son of William	July 22
338	William Woodberry son of Samˡˡ	
339	Joshua Pickard son of Jonathan	Aug. 5
340	Phinehas Hammond son of David junʳ	
341	Jane Scot Dʳ of Joseph junʳ	Aug. 12
342	Samuel Dresser son of Samˡˡ	Aug. 19
343	Hannah Elsworth Dʳ of Thomas	Sept. 2.
344	Joseph Pickard son of Joseph	
345	Sarah Kæsar Dᵗʳ of Moses	Sep. 23.
346	Hannah Pickard Dᵗʳ of Moses junʳ	Sep. 30
347	Joshua Prime son of Joshua	Oct. 14
348	Benjamin Todd son of John	
349	John Jewet son of John	Oct. 21
350	Mary Bayley Dᵗʳ of David	Nov. 4

351 Ann Jewet D. of Jonathan jun^r   Nov. 25
352 Caleb Cresey son of Abel } Dec. 9
353 Mary Barker D. of Jacob
354 Anne Bayley D. of Sam^ll   Dec. 23
355 Lydia Hobson D. of Moses   Feb. 17
356 Ruth Jewet D. of George   Feb. 24

      15 Males 17 Females.

1745

357 Mary Payson D. of Eliot   March 17
358 James Bayley son of James   March 24
359 Rebekah Jewet wife of James } Mar. 31
      Ipswich Adult
360 Daniel Clark son of Daniel
361 James Jewet son of James   May 27
362 Nathansel Brown son of widow } June 2
      Mary Brown baptized by M^r
      Chandler
363 John Sawyer son of Ezekiel   June 16
364 Eunice Duty D^r of Moses   June 23
365 Jonathan Jewet son of Jacob } July 7
366 Mary Kilborn D^r of Ebenezer
367 Jepththah & } Two negroe } Aug. 11
368 Lot } men
369 Jonathan Woodman son of } Sep. 1
      Joshua
370 Joseph Kilborn son of Joseph

371 Phinehas Dodge son of John } Sep. 29
372 Moses Palmer son of Stephen
373 Jeremiah Hidden son of Eben } Sep. 22
374 Aquila Jewet son of Amos
375 Ezekiel Cooper son of Leonard   Oct. 13
376 Sarah Jewet d^tr of James } 27
377 Rebekah Burpee da^tr of Joseph
378 Nathan Plats son of Nathan   Nov. 10
379 Deborah Gage da^tr of Thomas   Nov. 24
380 Jane Smith da^tr of Benj^m jun^r   Dec. 29
381 Jeremiah Todd son of Jeremiah   Dec. 22
382 Hannah Palmer da^tr of Daniel } Feb. 9
383 Paul Stickney son of William
384 Joseph Elswoith son of Jeremy } Feb. 23
      jun^r

      19 Males 9 Females

1746

385 Sarah Dickinson da^tr of James   March 2
386 Mary Hammond da^tr of David jun^r   March 9
387 Mary Todd da^tr of Jonathan
388 Edna Boynton da^tr of Ephraim } April 27
389 Jonathan Pickard son of Jon- } May 4
      athan
390 Bethiah Smith da^tr of Jonathan   May 7
391 Samuel Dresser son of Daniel } June 2
392 David Jewet son of Eliphalet

393 Hannah Hobson d^{tr} of Moses } July 13
394 James Jewet son of Mark
395 Jane Kilborn d^{tr} of Eliphalet — Aug. 17
396 Margaret Barker da^{tr} of Jacob — Aug. 24
397 Hannah Jewet D^r of Moses
398 Jane Pickard d^{tr} of Moses jun^r — Oct. 19
399 Mary Nelson D^r of David — Oct. 26
401 Hannah Johnson d^{tr} of Thomas — Nov. 2
402 Edward Chapman son of Edward — Dec. 7
403 Jacob Jewet son of Jacob — Jan. 4
404 Ezekiel Bayley son of David — Jan. 11
405 Enos Bishop son of Benjamin — Feb. 8
406 Mehetabel Hobson D^r of Humphry } Feb. 15
407 Elisabeth Jewet d^r of George } Feb. 22
408 Sarah Bayley d^r of Samuel

8 Males 15 Females

1747

409 Thomas Osborn son of John — Mar. 8
410 George Jewet son of John — March 22
411 John Jewet son of Jonathan
412 Edward Elsworth son of Thomas } March 29
413 Samuel Lowel son of Richard } April 19
414 Mehetabel Jewet D^r of Amos
415 Mehetabel Hidden D^r of Eben — May 24

416 Jeremiah Pickard son of Joseph — May 31
417 Joseph Sanders son of Edward Sanders jun^r } June 7
418 Thomas Hammond son of David jun^r } June 14
419 Ann Kilborn da^{tr} of Ebenezer — Aug. 9
420 Ruth Palmer da^{tr} of Stephen — Aug. 30
421
422 Moses Bayley son of James } Sep. 5. by Mr Chandler
423 Hannah Plats da^{tr} of Nathan }
424 Susanna Burpee da^{tr} of Isaac — Sep. 20
425 Joshua Prime son of Joshua — Sep. 20
426 Mark Duty son of Moses — Oct. 18
    Elisabeth Hibbert da^{tr} of James
427 Joseph Elsworth son of Jeremiah jun^r } Nov. 15
428 Lydia Dresser d^r of Daniel — Nov. 22
429 Sarah Dresser d^{tr} of Samuel
430 Job Boynton son of Ephraim — Jan. 10
431 Thomas Prime son of Thomas — Jan. 17
432 Eunice Wood da^{tr} of Thomas
433 Hannah Chaplin da^{tr} of John jun^r } Feb. 14
434 Sarah Cooper da^{tr} of Leonard — Feb. 28
435 Mark Pearson son of Jonathan } Feb. 28

15 Males 12 Females

1748

436	James Dickinson son of James	} March 7
437	Ephraim Pickard son of Jonathan	
438	Mary Burpee dar of Joseph	
439	Thomas Lambert son of Thomas	March 20
440	Apphia Gage dar of Thomas	April 3
441	Aquila Sawyer son of Ezekiel	April 17
442	Daniel Palmer son of Daniel	} May 1
443	Jonathan Jewet son of James	
444	Jeremiah Jewet son of Moses	June 12
445	John Bradstreet son of Nathanael	June 26
446	Elisabeth Brocklebank dar of Nathan	July 3
447	Lucey Stickney dar of William	July 17
448	William Jewet son of Jeremy junr	Sep. 11
449	Samuel Tenney son of Thomas	Sep. 25
450	Dinah dar of Lot and Ruth Mr Bradstreets servants	Oct. 16
451	Lydia Kilborn daughter of Joseph	Oct. 30
452	Jonathan Johnson son of Jonathan	Nov. 13

453	Elisabeth Hobson dar of Humphrey	} Nov. 20
454	Ebenezer Hidden son of Eben. by Mr Walley,	Nov. 27
455	Mehetabel Jewet dar of Mark	Dec. 11
456	Amos Pickard son of Moses	Feb. 5
457	Mary Tredwal Dr of Jonathan	Feb. 12
458	Joseph Jewet son of Jacob	Feb. 19
459	Daniel Jewet son of Jonathan	
460	Priscilla Scot dtr of Joseph junr	} Feb. 26
	15 Males 10 Females	

1749

461	Joseph Palmer son of Stephen	March 5
462	Joanna Jewet Dar of Eliphalet	March 12
463	Sarah Jewet dar of Thomas	Apr. 2
464	Lydia Saunders dar of Edward junr	April 9
465	Susanna Hammond dar of David junr	June 4
466	Mehetabel Burpee dar of Isaac	July 23
467	Solomon Lowel son of Richard	July 30
468	Jeremiah Elsworth son of Jeremiah junr	Sep. 3
469	Hannah Jewet dtr of John	Sep. 24

470 Mary Boynton da^{tr} of Ephraim — Oct. 8
471 Joanna Todd da^{tr} of Jeremiah — Oct. 15
472 William Duty son of Moses Duty — Jan. 14 and the first child Baptized in the new meeting-house

1750

473 Mehetabel Hidden da^{tr} of Eben — Feb. 11
474 Thomas Elsworth son of Thomas — Feb. 25
475 Susanna Bishop da^{tr} of Benjamin — March 4
476 Sarah Wood da^{tr} of Jonathan — March 18
477 John Spiller son of Samuel
6 Males 11 Females

478 Moses Wood son of Thomas jun^r — April 1
479 Amos Pearson son of Jonathan — April 29
480 Mary Pickard da^{tr} of Moses jun^r — May 13
481 George Jewet son of George — May 20
482 Sarah Palmer da^{tr} of Daniel
483 Mary Bradstreet da^{tr} of Nathanael — June 24
484 John Smith son of Jonathan & — June 24
485 Moses Jewet son of Moses
486 Caleb Jewet son of Jeremiah jun^r — July 15
487 Ezekiel Bradstreet son of Moses — Aug. 26
488 Lucey Nelson D^r of David — Sep. 30

489 Abigail Kilborn da^{tr} of Ebenezer — Oct. 14
490 Sarah Chapman da^{tr} of Edward — Dec. 2
491 Hannah Johnson da^{tr} of Jonathan — Dec. 30
492 Ruth Jewet da^{tr} of Purchase — Jan. 6
493 Elisabeth Dresser da^{tr} of David Dresser jun^r — Jan. 20
494 Lois Brocklebank da^{trs} of
495 Eunice Brocklebank — Nathan Gemini — Feb. 17
496 Mary Bayley daughter of Samuel — Feb. 24
497 Mehetabel Dresser da^{tr} of Daniel — March 3
498 John Johnson son of John — March 10
499 Elisabeth Jewet da^{tr} of Mark — March 24
8 Males 14 Females

1751

500 Moses Tenney son of Thomas — March 31
501 Jonathan Wood son of Jonathan — April 21
502 David Jewet son of Thomas — May 5
503 Jesse Cooper son of Leonard — May 12
504 Mary Hobson da^{tr} of Humphry
505 Mary Kilborn da^{tr} of Joseph — July 28
506 Hannibal son of Lot and Ruth
507 Samuel Elsworth son of Jeremiah jun^r — Aug. 11

508 Timothy Palmer son of John jun — Aug. 25
509 Paul Bayley son of James — Sep. 1
510 Lucey Lowel dau of Richard — Sep. 8
511 Hannah Spiller dau of Samuel — Nov. 17
    8 Males 4 Females

1752

512 Hannah Mighill dau of Thomas — Jan. 19
513 Mary Bayley dau of David — Feb. 16
514 Samuel–Northend Gage son of Nathanael } Mar. 1
515 Jonathan Todd son of Jeremiah } March 8
516 Nathan Smith son of Jonathan
517 Phoebe Jewet daughter of Jeremiah jun } April 5
518 William Gage son of Thomas — April 12
519 Abigail Sanders dau of Edward jun } April 19
520 William Todd son of Jonathan — May 24
— Moses Palmer son of Daniel — May 3
521 Abigail Pickard dau of Moses jun } June 7
522 Samuel Jewet son of Jacob
523 Dolly Scot dau of Saml Scot jun } June 14
524

525 Abigail Pearson dau of Jona- than } July 26
526 Sarah Palmer dau of Stephen — Aug. 2
527 Sarah Bradstreet dau of Nathanael } Oct. 1
528 Mary Stickney dau of Amos — Nov. 5
529 Abigail Prime dau of Thomas } Nov. 19
530 William Elsworth son of Thomas
531 Mary Pickard Dr of Jonathan — Dec. 10
532 Nathanael Jewet son of Moses — Dec. 24
    9 Males 12 Females

533   1753

534 Nathan Lambert son of Nathan — Jan. 7
535 Ruth Wood dau of Thomas } Feb. 4
536 Anne Kilborn dau of Ebenezer
537 Jane Jewet dau of John — March 11
538 Lydia Bishop daughter of Benjamin } April 22
539 Nathan Jewet son of Eliphalet — May 10
544 Jane Palmer dau of John — May 27
545 Hannah Mighil Dr of Nathanael } June 10
546 Moses Jewet son of Thomas
547 Susanna Dickinson dau John jun — June 24
548 Josiah Prime son of Joshua — July 22

549	Sarah Duty Dr of Moses	July 29
550	Nathanael Johnson son of John	
551	John Wood son of Jonathan	Aug. 12
552	Moses Richards son of Moses	Aug. 19
553	Joseph Brocklebank son of Nathan	
554	Anthony Nelson Twin son of David	Sep. 2
555	Joseph Tenny son of Thomas	Sep. 9
556	Hannah Smith dtr of Benjamin	
557	Thomas Kilborn son of Joseph	Sep. 30
558	Moses Bradstreet son of Moses	
559	Aaron Elsworth son of Jeremiah junr	Oct. 7
560	Susanna Cooper Dr of Leonard	Oct. 14
561	Sarah Jewet datr of Jeremiah junr	Nov. 25
562	Samuel Scots son Benjamin	Dec. 9
563	Hannah Bayley daughter of James	Dec. 23
564	Billey Price son of William	Dec. 30
565	Abiel Boynton son of Ephraim	Jan. 6
	17 Males 11 Females	
	1754	
566	John Page son of Nathanael	Feb. 3
567	Mehetabel Jewet datr of Mark	Feb. 10
568	Sarah Mighil datr of Thomas	Feb. 24
569	Patience Jewet datr of Purchis	April 14
570	Jeremiah Hobson son of William	April 21
571	Joseph Todd Twin son of Jeremiah	April 28
572	Elisabeth Sanders datr of Edward junr	June 2
573	Abijah Palmer son of Daniel	
574	John Pickard son of Moses junr	June 16
575	Sarah Lowel datr of Richard	July 14
576	Sarah Jewet datr of Eliphalet	Aug. 4
577	David Sterey son of Samuel	Aug. 25
578	Moses Hobson son of John	
579	Mehetabel Dickinson datr of John junr	Sep. 22
580	Susanna Palmer datr of Stephen	Sep. 23
581	Sarah Wood datr of Samuel	Oct. 27
582	Jonathan Pearson son of Jonatnan	
583	Scipio Jonathan Pickards servant Boy	Dec. 1
584	Hannah Lancaster datr of Thomas	Dec. 8
585	George Todd son of William	Dec. 15
586	William Palmer son of John ye 3rd	
	11 Males 10 Females	

1755

587 Cæsar Lots & Ruths child — Jan. 19
588 Martha Elsworth datr of Nathall — Feb. 16
589 Thomas Gage son of Thomas — March 2
590 Mary Clark datr of Moses — March 9
591 William Hale son of Doctr William Hale — Mar. 23
592 Ivory Kilborn son of Ebenezer — April 6
593 Mary Johnson datr of John — April 20
594 Daniel Jewet son of John — June 8
595 Sarah Pickard datr of Jonathan — June 29
596 Lucey Wood datr of Thos junr — July 13
— Mehetabel Prime datr of Joshua — Sep. 3 — born Aug. 29
597 Lucy Elsworth datr of Thomas — Sep. 28
598 Nathanael Bradstreet son of Moses — Oct. 5
599 John Prime son of Thomas — Oct. 12
600 Jane Jewet datr of Jeremiah tertius — Oct. 19
601 Benjamin Spiller son of Samll — Nov. 2
602 Benjamin Bishop son of Benj — Nov. 9
603 Susanna Todd dtr of Thomas
604 Humphry Hobson Richards son of Moses Richards — Nov. 23

605 Jane Plats
606 Hannah Plats } daughters of Mark Plats — Dec. 14
607 Abigail Plats

10 Males 11 Females

1756

608 Thomas Wood son of Samll — Feb. 1
609 Sarah Tenney datr of Thomas
610 Joshua Dickinson son of John junr — Feb. 29
611 Samuel Nelson son of David — March ye 7
612 John Pickard son of Samuel
613 Thomas Sanders son of Edward jun. — April 4
614 Nathan Palmer son of Daniel — May 2
615 Ruth Cromble datr of Benjamin
616 Betty Wood datr of Jonathan — May 9
617 Esther Dole datr of Nathan — May 16
618 Sarah Price datr of William — July 4
619 Benjamin Smith son of Benj. — July 11
620 Ruth Plats datr of Mark — Aug. 1
621 Joseph Palmer son of John ye 3d — Aug. 8
622 Betty Hale Dr of William — Nov.
623 Moses Pickard son of Moses junr — Nov. 14
624 Leonard Cooper son of Peter — Dec. 5

10 Males 7 Females

1757

625 Nathanael Hammond son of Oliver } Jan. 2

— David Elsworth son of Nathanael Feb. 6

626 Hannah Palmer datr of John junr } Feb. 13

627 Nathanael Bradstreet son of Moses

628 Sarah Pearson datr of Jonathan Feb. 20

629 Samuel Lancaster sn of Thomas Mar. 13

630 Daniel Todd son of William Mar. 20

631 Humphry Hobson son of Humphry } Mar. 27

632 John Scot son of Samuel junr

633 Samuel Bayley son of Samuel May 8

634 Dorcas Kilborn } Twin daughters of Ebenezer Kilborn } May 22

635 Elisabeth Kilborn

636 Jane Clark datr of Moses July 31

637 Nathanel Mighil son of Nathall junr } Sept. 4.

638 Bridget Prime datr of Joshua Sep. 11.

639 Abigail Jewet datr of Moses Aug. 28

640 Hannah Hobson datr of William Sep. 18

641 Paul Johnson son of John } Oct. 2

642 David Lambert son of Nathan

643 Elisabeth Burpee datr of Joseph } Oct. 9

644 Amoz Todd son of Thomas

645 Elisabeth Cresey datr of Mark Oct. 30

646 Edward Payson son of James

647 Lydia Palmer datr of Stephen } Dec. 25

648 Jeremiah Jewett son of Jeremiah

649 Elisabeth Bray datr of Enoch

14 Males 11 Females

1758

650 William Bayley sn of William Feb. 12

651 Dolly Dickinson datr of John junr } March 12

652 Susanna Jewett datr of John April the 2d

653 Mary Hopkinson datr of Moses

654 Gideon Wood son of Samuel April 18

655 Sarah Todd datr of James

656 John Dresser son of John } May 21

657 Amos Wood sn of Thos junr May 29

658 Joanna Pickard datr of Jonathan July 9

659 Samuel Pickard son of Samuel Dec. 10

660 Paul Todd son of Thomas Nov. 26

6 Males 5 Females

1759

661 William Hobson son of William ⎱ Jan. 7
    liam

662 Ezekiel Lancaster son of Paul   Jan. 21

663 Patience Palmer daᵗʳ of John ⎱ Feb. 4
    junʳ

664 Josiah Stickney son of Jonathan Feb. 18

665 Hannah Barker daᵗʳ of Joseph   Feb. 25

666 Elisabeth Pearson daᵗʳ of Jon- ⎱ March 11
    athan

667 Elisebeth Palmer daᵗʳ of John
    yᵉ 3ᵈ

668 Sarah Hammond daᵗʳ of Sarah   April 1

669 David Payson son of James   May 6

670 Sarah Wood daᵗʳ of Jonathan   May 20

671 Priscilla Lancaster daᵗʳ of Thoˢ June 3

672 Josiah Stickney son of Moses   June 17

673 William Todd son of William   July 22

674 Amos Parsons son of Amos ⎱ Aug. 26
675 Rebekah Parsons daᵗʳ of An-
    drew

676 Martha Hale daᵗʳ of William   Sep. 2

677 Nathaniel Mighill son of Jere- ⎱ Sep. 9
    miah

678 Joseph Brocklebank son of Na- ⎱ Oct. 21
    than

679 Mehetabel Burpee daᵗʳ of ⎱ Oct. 28
    Joseph
680 Jacob Elsworth son of Na-
    thanael

681 Abigail Dresser daᵗʳ of John   Dec. 9

682 Lydia Pickard daᵗʳ of Moses ⎱ Dec. 23
    junʳ

        10 Males & 12 Females

        1760

683 Stephen Palmer son of Stephen Jan. 13

684 John Dole son of Nathan ⎱ Feb. 10
685 Mary Lancaster dᵗʳ of Paul

686 Samuel Hidden son of Price   Feb. 24

687 Jane Gage daᵗʳ of Nathanael   March 2

688 Elisabeth Jewet daᵗʳ of Jer- ⎱ March 23
    emiah
689 George Bayley son of William

690 Susanna Wood daᵗʳ of Samuel   April 6

691 Elisabeth Jewet Dʳ of Moses   April 20

692 Elisabeth Nelson daᵗʳ of David ⎱ April 27
693 Samuel Spiller son of Samuel

694 Lucey Bradstreet daᵗʳ of Moses   May 4

695 Mercy Smith daᵗʳ of Benjamin   June 8

696 Hannah Payson daᵗʳ of Edward ⎱ Aug. 3
    junʳ

697 Ephraim Hidden son of Ephraim Aug. 24
698 Paul Jewet son of Paul
699 Elisabeth Hopkinson datr of Moses
700 Joshua-Jewet Prime son of Joshua } Nov. 16
701 Thomas Todd son of Thomas Nov. 23
 9 males & 10 females

1761

702 Mary Howe datr of Mark Jan 18
703 Moses Johnson son of John
704 Elisabeth Saunders datr of Humphry } Feb 1
706 Asa Low sn of Jacob March 15
707 Elisabeth Payson datr of James Apr. 19
708 William Hobson Sn of William
709 Phebe Dresser datr of Daniel junr } May 3
710 Susanna Dickinson datr of John junr } May 31
711 Stephen Pearson son of Jonathan } June 7
712 William Rutherford sn of William } June 21
713 Joseph Barker son of Joseph
714 Moses Clark son of Moses } July 5

715 Mehetabel Lambert datr of Thomas } July 26
716 Moses Todd son of William
717 Benjamin Dresser son of John
718 Mehetabel Mighill datr of Jeremiah } Aug. 2
719 John Phillips sn of James Aug. 23
720 David Payson son of Eliot junr Aug. 30
721 Mary Hale datr of William Sep. 13
722 Elisabeth Pickard datr of Moses Sep. 20
724 Hannah Cooper son of James Oct. 4
725 Samuel Pearson son of Samll Sep. 27
726 Ruth Winter datr of Benjanin Dec. 6
 12 males & 11 females

1762

727 Eunice Jewett datr of Jeremiah Jan. 3
728 Mehetabel Cresey datr of Mark
729 Elizabeth Palmer datr of Francis junr } Jan. 10
730 Northend Cogswell son of Doctor Nathanael Cogswell } Feb. 14
731 Mary Wood datr of Samuel Feb. 21
732 Adoniram Hedden son of Ephraim } March 21
733 Mary Palmer datr of John the 3d March 28

734	Mehetabel Hedden da^{tr} of Price	April 18
735	Sarah Sanders da^{tr} of William	May 2
736	Hannah Bradstreet da^{tr} of Moses	} June 27
737	Mary Elsworth da^{tr} of Nathaniel	
738	Molly Cooper da^{tr} of Peter deceased	Aug. 22
739	Mehetabel Todd da^{tr} of James	Sep. 12
740	Ephraim Brown son of Francis	Nov. 14
741	Bridget Prime da^{tr} of Joshua	Nov. 21
742	Sarah Lancaster da^{tr} of Thomas	Dec. 26
	3 males & 13 females	

1763

743	Joshua Sanders son of Humphry	} Jan. 9
744	Dudley Stickney son of David	
745	Hannah Stickney da^{tr} of Moses	Jan. 16
746	Mehetabel Bayley da^{tr} of John	Jan. 23
747	William Sanders } Gemini: of	
748	Anne Sanders } William	} Feb. 13
749	Jacob Pickard son of Jacob	
750	John Barker son of Thomas	Mar. 13
751	Sarah Cogswell da^{tr} of Nathanael	June 12
752	Aaron Wood son of Jonathan	June 26

753	Joshua Davis son of James	} July 3
754	Tabitha Pearson da^{tr} of Jonathan	
755	Sarah Jewett da^{tr} of Moses	July 17
756	Jacob Smith son of Benjamin	
757	Jonathan Stickney son of Jonathan	} July 31
758	John Hammond } Children	
759	Sarah Hammond	of David
760	Joanna Hammond } Hammond	} Aug. the 7
761	David Hammond	Junior
762	Mary Payson da^{tr} of James	
763	Joshua Todd son of Thomas	
764	Mary Dresser da^{tr} of John	} Aug. 14
765	Mary Jewett da^{tr} of Paul	
766	Moses Hale sⁿ of William	Aug. 21
767	Moses Pickard son of Moses	Sep. 4
768	Sarah Mighll da^{tr} of Jeremiah	
769	Elisabeth Bradstreet da^{tr} of Natha^{ll}	} Sep. 11
770	Lucey Pickard da^{tr} of Jonathan	
771	Mary Todd da^{tr} of William	} Sep. 18
772	Daniel Searl son of David	
773	Hannah Johnson da^{tr} of John	
774	Rose Mrs Hibbertts negroe Girl	} Oct. 9
775	Lydia Clark da^{tr} of Moses	Oct. 23

776 Peter Cooper son of James — Nov. 20
777 Jonathan Lambert son of Thos — Dec. 4
778 Stephen-Hunt Bagley son of Abel — Dec 18

18 males 18 females

1764

779 Samuel Dresser son of Samuel — Jan. 1
780 Edward Sanders son of John — Jan. 29
781 Lois Jewett datr of Jeremiah — } Feb. 5.
782 Sarah Cresey datr of James
783 Daniel Palmer son of Francis junr — } Feb. 26
784 Molley Wood datr of Samuel — April 15
786 Lois Palmer datr of John
787 Alexander Rutherford son of William — } July 15
788 Hannah Low datr of Jacob — Aug. 19
789 Jacob Elsworth son of Nathanael — } Aug. 26
790 Elisabeth Cogswell datr of Nathanll
791 Jonathan Hidden son of Ephraim — Sept. 16
792 James Todd sn of James — Nov. 11
793 Oliver Prime sn of Joshua — } Nov. 18
794 Stephen-Woodman Hunt sn of Stuart Hunt

795 Elisabeth Palmer datr of Samuel — Nov. 25

9 males 7 Females

1765

796 Nathanael Lambert son of Thomas — } Feb. 17
797 Eunice Hidden datr of Price — March 10
798 Mary Hale datr of Doctr William — Mar. 31
799 Elias Bagley son of Abel — April 14
800 Isaac Davis son of James — April 21
801 Ellis Cooper sn of James
802 Eliot Sawyer sn of Ezekiel junr — } May 12
803 Moses Todd sn of Thomas
804 Aaron Palmer sn of Francis — } July 7
805 Daniel Dresser son of John — July 14
806 Thomas Mighll sn of Jeremiah — July 21
807 Elisabeth Lowel datr of Moses — July 28
808 Nathanael Cogswell sn of Nathll — Aug. 11
809 James Payson son of James — Aug. 25
810 Joseph Sanders sn of William — Sep. 1
811 Dorothy Bradstreet datr of Moses — } Sep. 8
812 Nathan Jewett sn of Stephen junr
813 Moses Cresey sn of James — } Sep. 15

814 David Bradstreet sn of Nathanael — Sep. 29
815 Daniel-Clark Hobson sn of David — Oct. 6.
816 Joseph Smith sn of Benjamin — Oct. 20
817 Andrew Hobson sn of William — Nov. 3
818 Sarah Stickney datr of Jonathan — Nov. 24
819 Elisabeth Todd datr of William — Dec. 1
820 Priscilla Dresser datr of Samll — Dec. 15

18 males 7 Females

1766

821 Aaron Clark son of Moses
822 Sarah Jewett datr of Purchase junr — Feb. 23
823 Andrews Palmer sn of Paul — March 9
824 Ruth Jewett datr of Paul
825 Margaret Wood datr of Samuel — March 23
826 Mary Rutherford datr of William — April 6
827 Ebenezer Hidden sn of Ephraim — April 27
828 David Sanders son of John
829 Jeremiah Harris son of Timothy — May 25
830 Moses Wood sn of Jonathan — June 8
831 Pierce Bayley sn of John junr — July 13

832 Sarah Hunt datr of Stuart — July 27
833 Dorothy Hale datr of Doctor William — Aug. 3
834 David Searl son of David — Sep. 7
835 Ezekiel Sanders sn of Humphry — Sep. 21
836 Joseph Bagley son of Abel — Sep. 28
837 Nathanael Cogswell son of Doctor Nathll — Oct. 5
838 Edward Palmer sn of Samll — Oct. 19
839 Sarah Todd datr of David — Nov. 9
840 William Cresey sn of Abel — Dec. 7
841 Thomas Pickard sn of Thomas — Dec. 14

14 Males 7 females

1767

842 Ruth Jewett datr of Stephen junr — Feb. 1
—   Hannah Elsworth datr of Nathanael — Jan.
843 Joanna Jewett datr of Purchase junr — Feb. 8
844 Mark Cresey son of Mark
845 Susanna Bailey datr of John — May 3
846 Mary Jewett datr of Jeremiah
847 Elisabeth Scott datr of Samll junr — May 10

848	Hannah Todd dat^r of Asa	May 24
849	Mary Pickard dat^r of Sam^ll	June 7
850	Mary Harris dat^r of John jun^r	June 28
851	Mehetabel Bayley dat^r of Deacon Bayley	} July 12
852	Nathan Dresser son of John Dresser	
853	Eliot Payson son of James	Aug. 23
854	Sarah Kilborn dat^r of Daniel	Sep. 6
855	Hannah Todd dat^r of William	Sep. 20
856	John Cresey son of John	Sep. 27
857	Martha Hidden d^r of Price	} Nov. 15
858	Hannah Cogswell dat^r of Nathanael	
859	Dorothy Dresser dat^r of Samuel	} Dec. 13
860	Joseph Rutherford son of William	

14 Females and 5 Males y^s year

1768

861	Nehemiah Jewett s^n of Nehemiah jun^r	} Jan. 10
862	Jonathan Plummer son of Sam^ll	
863	Ezekiel Sawyer son of Ezekiel	Jan. 17
864	Jedidiah Barker s^n of Nathanael	Jan. 24
865	Nathaniel Prime s^n of Joshua	} Jan. 31
866	Nathaniel Todd s^n of Thomas	
867	Sarah Palmer d^r Francis jun^r	} Feb. 14
868	Jacob Cresey son of Abel	
869	Dorothy Pickard dat^r of Joshua	} Mar. 13
870	Daniel Bradstreet son of Nathaniel	
871	Jonathan Bradstreet son of Moses	
872	Henry Warrin son of Henry	} April 10
873	Elisabeth Stickney dat^r of Jonathan	
874	Stephen Hunt s^n of Stuart	April 17
875	Sarah Cresey dat^r of James	} May 1
876	Timothy Harris son of Timothy	
877	Hannah Lowel dat^r of Moses	May 15
878	Lydia Hobson dat^r of William	May 22
879	Hannah Hidden dat^r of Ephraim	} June 26
880	Abigail Pickard dat^r of Thomas	
881	Thomas Dickinson s^n of Moses	July 17
882	Joseph Jewett son of Joseph	Aug. 28
883	Joshua Jewett son of Paul	} Sep. 25
884	Sarah Cresey dat^r of John	

885	Thomas Palmer son of Sam^ll	Oct. 9
886	Mary Sanders dat^r of John	Oct. 23
887	Sarah Payson dat^r of James	Dec. 10
	16 males 11 Females	

1769

888	Mary Jewett dat^r of Nehemiah	Jan. 8
889	Bradstreet Hale son of William	Jan. 22
890	Jonathan Todd son of James	Feb. 26
891	Sarah Jewett dat^r of Purchase	March 12
892	Susanna Jewett dat^r of Jeremiah	Mar. 19
893	Jane Tenney dat^r of Benjamin	April 9
894	Dudley Todd s^n of Asa	
895	Deborah Payson dat^r of Moses-Paul	April 23
897	Ann Dresser dat^r of John	
898	Wade Cogswell son of Nathaniel	June 25
899	Edna Todd dat^r of William	Oct. 15
900	Salome Bayley dat^r of John	Oct. 29
901	Samuel Plummer son of Samuel	
902	Mary Scott dat^r of Moses	
903	Mary Sawyer dat^r of Ezekiel	Dec. 3^d
904	Jenny Todd (so called by her Father) dat^r of John jun^r	

905	Abel Cresey son of Abel	Dec. 17
906	Phœbe Harris dat^r of John jun^r	Dec. 31
	6 Males 12 Females	

1770

907	Sarah Pickard dat^r of Samuel	Jan. 21
908	Elisabeth Perley dat^r of John	Feb. 11
909	Elisabeth Todd dat^r of Thomas	Feb. 25
910	Mary Harris dat^r of Timothy	
911	Mary Pickard dat^r of Joshua	April 8
912	Elisabeth Sawyer dat^r of John	
913	a daughter of Nehemiah Jewett jun^r whom he called Jenny	April 15
914	Abner-Ross Bayley } Sons of	
915	Amos Bayley } Amos Bayley	May 6
916	Nathan Bradstreet son of Nathanael	May 13
917	Nathanael Barker son of Nathanael	June 3
918	Ebenezer Jewett son of Stephen jun^r	June 10
919	Richard Cresey son of John	July 8
920	Edward Jewett son of Aaron	July 22
921	Hannah Safford dat^r of Daniel	
922	Joseph Kilborn son of Joseph jun^r	July 29

923	Mary Dresser da^tr of Samuel }	Aug. 12
924	John-Pemberton Palmer son of Francis jun^r	
925	John Jewett son of Joseph	Sep. 16
926	Daniel Green son of Thomas }	Sep. 9
927	Ezekiel Bayleys da^tr which he called by the nickname Betty	
928	Elisabeth Pearson da^tr of Samuel	Oct. 7
929	Abigail Cogswell da^tr of Nathanael }	Oct. 21
930	Jonathan Searl son of David	Nov. 18
931	Charlotte Jewett da^tr of Nehemiah Jewett }	Dec. 2
932	Joanna Todd da^tr of David Todd	
933	Lydia Bayley da^tr of Amos }	Dec. 16
934	Moses-Paul Payson son of Moses-Paul	
935	John Sanders son of John	Dec. 23
	14 males 15 Females	
	1771	
936	Rhode Jewett da^tr of Deac. Jeremiah }	Jan. 13
937	Apphia Stickney da^tr of Jonathan	
38	—— Martin son of Nathanael	
939	Joseph Scott son of Moses	March 10
940	Jane Payson da^tr of James }	March 17
941	Jane Jewett da^tr of Paul	
942	Amos Cresey son of James	March 24
943	Thomas Bayley son of John	April 7
944	Mary Todd da^tr of Daniel jun^r	June 28
945	Purchase Jewett son of Purchase }	Aug. 11
946	Mary Tenny da^tr of Benjamin	
947	Humphry Sanders son of Humphry	Sep. 8
948	William-Price Hidden son of Price }	Oct. 13
—	Jonathan Pickard son of Joshua	
949	Dorothy Cogswell da^tr of Nathaniel }	Dec. 15
950	Jeremiah Jewett son of Nehemiah	
951	A daughter of John Cresey	Dec. 29
	7 males 9 females	
	1772	
952	Sarah Jewett da^tr of George jun^r }	Jan. 12
953	Sarah Bradstreet da^tr of John	Feb. 2

954	Ebenezer Jewett son of Stephen	Feb. 16
955	Joseph Todd son of Nelson	
956	Aaron Jewett son of Aaron	
957	Benjamin Sawyer son of John	Feb. 23
958	Patience Jewett datr of Ephraim	
959	John-March Stickney sn of Jonathan	March 1
960	John Harris son of Timothy	May 3
961	David Rutherford son of William	
962	Bradstreet Plummer son of Samll	June 21
963	Moses Sawyer son of Moses	June 28
964	Jedidiah Todd son of John	
965	Moses Todd son of William	July 5
966	David Jewett son of Joseph	
977	William Lambert son of Thomas junr	July 26
978	Soloman Todd son of Thomas	
979	Abraham Jewett son of Nehemiah junr	Aug. 30
980	Hannah Perley datr of John	Sep. 6
981	Elisabeth Kilborn datr of Joseph junr	Oct. 28
982	Lois Bayley datr of Ezekiel	Nov. 8
983	Jonathan Jewett son of David	Dec. 5

16 males 6 females

1773

984	Phebe Bradstreet datr of Nathanael	Jan. 3
985	Thomas Safford son of Daniel	
986	Elisabeth Dresser datr of Joseph	Jan. 10
987	Anna Bayley datr of John	
988	Thomas Elsworth son of Thos junr	
989	Mehetabel Barker datr of Nathanael	Jan. 24
990	Elisabeth Sanders datr of John	
991	Aaron Palmer son of Francis junr	Feb. 7
992	Mehetabel Sawyer datr of Ezekiel	
993	John Sawyer sn of John	April 4
994	Ephraim Jewett sn of Ephraim	
995	Eliot Payson sn of Moses-Paul	Apr. 11
996	Mary Pickard datr of Ephraim	Apr. 25
997	Elisabeth Mighill datr of Jeremiah	May 23

998	Susanna Jewett daᵗʳ of George junʳ	} June 6
999	Anna Todd daᵗʳ of James	June 27
1000	Jane Todd daᵗʳ of Daniel	
1001	Judith Bradstreet daᵗʳ of John	} July 25
1002	Abigail Bradstreet daᵗʳ of Ezekiel	
1003	Lydia Tenny daᵗʳ of Benjamin	Aug. 1
1004	Elisabeth Todd daᵗʳ of Asa	Aug. 8
1005	Caleb Searl son of David	Aug. 23
1006	Edna Jewett daᵗʳ of Paul	
1007	Eliot Payson son of James	Sep. 5
1009	Hannah a negro woman	Oct. 17
1000	Nathanael Jewett son of Stephen	Oct. 31
1001	Elisabeth Jewett daᵗʳ of Moses junʳ	} Nov. 7
1002	Abigail Todd daᵗʳ of John	Nov. 21
1003	Abigail Jewett daᵗʳ of Aaron	Dec. 12

Males 9 Females 20

1774

1004	Mary Lancaster daᵗʳ of Thoˢ junʳ	} Jan. 9

1004	Nathanael Harris son of Timothy	} Feb. 27
1005	Caleb Jewett son of Nehemiah	
1006	Elisabeth Lambert daᵗʳ of Thomas junʳ	} March 6
1009	John Hidden son of Price	March 27

Thomas Mighill Clerk

_____

1	Amos Pickard son of Samuel	June 19
2	Mary Dresser Dresser Daughter of Joseph	} July 10
3	Elisabeth Todd Daughter of Benjamin	
4	Amos Dresser son of Amos	July 17
5	Lucy-Gage Daughʳ Samuel-Northend Gage	} August 7ᵗʰ 1774
	Jedediah Jewett son of David Baptized By Mʳ Lesle	Aug. 14
6	Mary Bailey daughter of John	
7	Hannah Jewett daughter of George junʳ	} Oct. 30
8	Ruth Jewett daughter of Ephraim	
9	Abigail Pickard Daughter of Ephraim	

10 Hannah Scot Daughter of Moses } Decr 11
11 Moses Pickard son of Jeremiah Pickard

1775

12 Joseph Sanders son of John } Janu. 15
13 Sarah Jewett Daughter of Moses } Feb. 5th
14 Elisabeth Sawyer Dag^r of Ezekiel & Mary } March 5th
15 Thomas Payson son of Moses-Paul Payson & Deborah his wife
16 Sewell Pearson son of Nathan
17 Thomas Green son of Thomas Green Baptised } March 19

1776

Solomon Lowell son of Solomon } Janu. 10
Hannah Gage Daug^r of William Gage
Dolle Bradstreet Daug^r of Moses jun^r
Mary Street D. Nathaniel } Feb. 18

David Dresser S. of Amos
Appea Lambert D. of Thomas } March 18
Elizebeth Todd D. Benjamin } April
Elizebeth Martin D. Nathaniel May 12
Eliphelet Jewett son of Paul
Benjamin Tenney S. Benjamin
William-Spafard Jewett S. Ephraim
Thomas Jewett S. Nehemiah } June 2
Stephen Harris S. Timothy
Elisabeth Sanders D. John } July 1776
Jane Pickard D. Ephraim
Sarah Pickard D Joshua
Jeremiah Jewett S. Aaron
Ester Hammond D. Thomas } August
Mehitabel Payson D. James
Nathaniel Elsworth S. Thomas
Luca Jewett D. George } Sept. 1776
Elizabeth Gage D Sam-Nor-Gage
Ruth Pearson D. John J^r } Dec. 1776

1777

Hannah Jewett D. Stephen } Jan. 1777
John Bailey S. John

Caleb Todd S. Nathan
Joseph Sawyer S. Ezekiel
David Payson S. Moses-Paul } April 13th
Moses Jewett S. Moses jun.
Betty Pearson D. Nathan
Sarah Bradstreet D. Moses jun.

Judith Pearly D. John } Aug. 3
Sarah Jewett D. Ephraim

Joseph Hale S. Dr William } Oct. 5
Daniel Todd s. Daniel jun.
John Bailey S. John of Manchester

Jonn Sawyer S. John } Oct. 26
Hannah Bradstreet D. John
John Hammond S. Thomas
Jacob Lowell S. Solomon

1778

Moses Kilborn son of Joseph junr } Feb. 1
Elizabeth Gage D. of Hannah widow of William Gage } Feb. 8
Thomas Lambert S. Thomas   Feb. 15
Ephraim Hidden S. Price } March 1
Sarah Jewett D. David

Hannah Jewett D. Aaron
Prudence Jewett D. Jacob
Ezra Martin S. Nathaniel } March 15
Nathaniel Safford S. Daniel
Lucy Bailey D. Amos } April 12 by Mr Noble
Sarah Pearson D. John junr
Nathaniel Cogswell son of Nathaniel

Eunice Bailey D. Ezekiel } May 3 by Mr Dana
Jeminah Bradstreet } Ds Eze-
Salla Bradstreet } kiel

Elisabeth Sawyer D. Moses } July 12 by Mr Rogers
Ruth Pickard D. Joshua
Hannah Dresser D. Amos
Wallingford Todd S. Benjamin } Sept. 6

Elisabeth Jewett D. Stephen } Novr 8
Mehetabel Pickard Daugr of Jeremiah

Joseph Bishop S. Edward   Dec. 22
Mehitabel Pickard D. Jeremiah Oct.
Moses Bradstreet S. Moses jun. Dec. 30

1779

Daniel Harris S. Timothy } Jan. 3
Dolly Sanders D. John

Josiah Plummer S. Samuel } Jan. 10
Susey Cleves D. Nathaniel
Samuel Gage S.Sam.-Nor.-Gage Feb. 14
Hannah Todd D. Nathan }
Paul Elsworth S. Thomas Feb. 28
Elisabeth Pickard D. Ephraim Feb. 28
Anna Lambert D. Thomas March 21
Dolly Green D. Thomas
John Lambert S. Nathan } April 4
Asa Jewett S. Purchase Jr
Nathaniel Bradstreet S. Na- } May 2
thaniel
Anne Sawyer D. Ezekiel May 16
Lois Cogswell D. of Dr Nathll June 27
Dolly Jewett D. George
Priscilla Pearley D. John } July 4
Joseph Bailey son John
Thomas Sawyer S. John } July 25
Mehetabel Jewett D. Jacob Aug. 15
Joseph Jewett S. Nehemiah Oct. 4
Elisabeth Mighill D. Thomas Nov. 15
John Barker S. Nathanael }
Benjamin Lowell S. Solomon } Dec. 5

1780
Nathaniel Todd S. George Jan. 30
Abigail Pearson D. Nathan April 16

Paul Jewett S. Paul }
Moses Jewett S. Aaron
Benjamin Todd S. Benjamin
Thomes Kilborn S. Joseph junr
John Dow S. John } May 28
David Jewett S. David
Joseph } Jewet S. Moses
Jeremiah } junr
ElisabethPearson D. John junr
Sally Saford D. Daniel Sept. 10
David Bailey S. Ezekiel Sept. 27
Hannah Pickard D. Joshua }
Eunice Sawyer D. Moses Oct. 8
Dorothy Cogswell D. Dr Nathl Oct. 29
Lucy Bradstreet D. Moses junr Dec. 3
James Whorff S. James Dec. 31

1781
Joseph Sanders S. John Jan. 14
Elisabeth Plummer D. Samuel }
Amos Pickard S. Jeremiah March 11
Hannah Elsworth D. Thomas }
Sarah Jewett D. Jacob April 29
Rebekah Kilborn D. John }
Hannah Jewett D. David July 1
Nathaniel-Mighill Pearly S. } July 8
John

Dorothy Mighill D. Thomas ⎫ Aug. 19
Charity Bailey D. John ⎬
Thomas Lambert S. Thomas ⎭ Sept. 16
Sarah Bradstreet D.Nathaniel ⎫ Nov. 25
Mary Payson D. Moses-Paul ⎭

1782.

Nathaniel Bailey S. Amos
Jane Sawyer D. Ezekiel
Elisabeth Smith D. Isaac ⎬ March 10
Henery-Bailey Todd S. Nel-
son
Joseph Jewett S. Joseph ⎫ April 14
Jonathan Jewett S. Aaron ⎬ Sept. 7
Jonathan Cogswell S. Dr Nathl
—— Pearson X Nathan

1783

Jacob-Pierson Bradford S. ⎫ Feb. 27
Rev. Mr Bradford ⎬
—— Kilborn X Joseph
Betsey Johnston
Susa Searl Johnston ⎬ March 9
Rachel Johnston
Benjamin Dresser Wharf S. ⎫ May 11
James ⎭
Debar Medchief Johnston ⎫ June 15
child Samuel
John Pickard ⎬ July 11
Polly Pearly ⎫ Gemini
Sally Pearly ⎬ Sept. 3
Anna Mighill D. Thomas ⎫ Dec. 7
Sarah Pickard ⎭
Carried to the new Book

Church Record Index

All names appearing in the church records have been indexed here. Women are listed by both maiden and married names where given. The spelling given in the text has been retained in the index. This results in some bizarre spellings by modern standards, and has been aggravated by the fact that the text frequently uses "f" in place of "s" according to the old style. Thus, readers are advised to spend some time browsing through the index in search of peculiar name variations.

103 251 252 Mary 102 103
107 247 251 Miriam 91 103
Nathan 105 255 Prifcilla
254 Samuel 105 255 Tho
102
BISHOP, Benj 288 Benjamin
274 281 283 285 286 288
Edward 281 301 Enos 283
Jemima 276 Joseph 301
Josiah 273 274 276 Lydia
91 273 286 Mary 281
Susanna 285
BLAKE, Joanna 110 Lyman H
78
BLODGETTE, George B 77 273
BOFWELL, Br 208 Mary 208
BOINTON, Abiel 226 Abraham
225 228 243 Ann 206 209
Anne 89 Benjamin 223
Bennoni 210 Benoni 100
228 243 Birthiah 244
Bithiah 89 106 Bridget 86
104 220 224 226 Bridgett
91 Caleb 81 82 85 98 206-
210 212 214 217 Capt 84
Daniel 215 216 David 224
Dorothy 91 105 243
Ebenezer 214 Ebenezr 246
Edna 106 245 Eleazar 220
Elifabeth 246 Elleonar
102 Eleonr 248 Ellin 215
Ephraim 228 Ephrim 105
Hannah 84 106 207 217 219
228 Hephziba 210 Hilkiah
89 101 213 246 248-252
Iccabod 208 Jane 209 251
Jeremiah 212 Jerufha 246
Jno 99 246 Jofeph 82 215
221 223 228 243 246 248
Jofeph Jr 86 220 245
Jofhua 219 Jofhuah 209
211 215 Johanna 246 John
89 207-209 211 243 244
246 249 Jonathan 209 212
Joseph 81 205-210 212 213
221 224 226 Joseph Jr 217
218 Margaret 98 208 Mary
82 83 105 217 243
Mehetable 252 Mofes 228
Nathan 226 Nathaniel 218
Prifcilla 89 101 246

Richard 99 207 224 226
Ruth 88 99 210 250 Samll
85 220 223 228 243 Samuel
84 214-218 225 228 245
Samuell 218 Sarah 205 217
228 243 245 249 Stephen
223 243 William 81 82 98
206 215 Zacharias 248
Zachery 215 Zacheus 105
243
BOREBANCK, Caleb 213
Ebenezer 213
BOREBANK, Caleb 83 205-211
Eliezar 210 Goodm Jr 205
John 206 Liddeah 82
Martha 209 Mary 207
Samuel 211 Timothy 208
BOREBANKE, John 203 Mary
203
BOYNTON, Abiel 287 Amos
280 Bethiah 93 Dea 110
Edna 282 Elifabeth 94 110
Elisabeth 274 Ephraim 94
274-276 279-283 285 287
Hannah 93 Hilkiah 101 243
Isaac 222 Jane 243
Jedidiah 281 Job 283 John
276 Mary 285 Ruth 97
Samuel 222 Sarah 279
BRADFORD, Bethiah 95
Ebenezer 77 97 Jacob-
Pierson 303
BRADFTREET, Aaron 209
Abigail 103 116 251
Bridget 219 Bridgett 208
Br 217 Dorithy 217
Elizabeth 214 217 Ezekiel
116 Goodw 82 Hannah 84 85
92 94 206 218 220 Humphy
220 Jane 104 228 Jno 220
John 96 114 216 217 222
Jonathan 215 Lucy 95 Mary
104 Mof 85 Mofes 82 83 95
103 111 206-210 213 214
216 218 219 221 222 227
228 254 Mofes Jr 104 251
Moses 96 205 Nathanael 94
114 227 Nathaniel 205
Nathanl 254 Nathanll 104
Nathll 92 96 Phebe 96
Phoebe 114 Ruth 95 Samuel

Hannah 115 253 James 83
99 109 209 210 225 227
247 Jno 252 Jofeph 228
John 98 103 253 254 John
Jr 112 114 Martha 89 100
Mary 225 Mehetabel 114
Mercy 98 Mrs 108 Mofes 97
115 Rebecca 244 Ruth 100
Samuel 100 210 228 Sarah
227 253 Sufanna 103 Tho
98 104 Tho Jr 254 Thomas
97 222 224 228 252 253
Thomas Jr 252 Thos 115
DICKINSON, Amos 281 Daniel
278 David 279 Dolly 289
Elisabeth 275 George 275
277-279 281 James 280-282
284 Jane 276 Jeremiah 275
277 John 273 274 John Jr
286-289 291 Joshua 274
288 Mehetabel 287 Moses
281 295 Paul 280 Sarah
278 282 Susanna 286 291
Thomas 274 278 295 Thomas
Jr 275 276 William 273
274
DODGE, Kezia 110 John 282
Phinehas 282
DOLE, Amos 252 Enoch 92
255 Esther 288 John 290
Joseph 255 Nathan 112 288
290 Phoebe 112 Rachel 92
Richard 102 248 249 252
Sarah 109 248 Stephen 249
DONNEL, Elifabeth 102
DONNELL, Benjamin 246
Nathanll 246
DORMAN, Ephraim 210 Hannah
210 Phebe 211 Seth 211
DOW, Benjamin 245 Daniel
254 Hephzibah 274
Jeremiah 104 253-255
Jeremy 274 Jno 246 John
245 302 Mofes 246 William
253
DOWNES, Elizabeth 216
Richard 216
DOWNING, Jonathan 273 275
Priscilla 273
DREFER, Abigail 215
Benjamin 215 Bethiah 97

Elizabeth 84 212 Henery
216 Jeremiah 213 Jno 99
John 204 211 212 John Jr
215 216 218 Liddiah 211
Lideah 216 Margaret 99
Mary 204 Mehitable 218
Mercy 84 Samuel 84 97 208
211 213 215 216 Thomas
208 211
DREFFER, see DREFER
DREFSER, Aaron 106 Amos
245 Benjamin 246 Br 81
Daniel 92 94 105 224
Daniel Jr 113 David 97
226 243 David Jr 109 Edna
255 Elifabeth 247
Elizabeth 205 Hannah 107
111 210 244 247 James 222
252 Jane 104 208 228
Jeremiah 243 Jno 85 Jno
Jr 220 222 253 Jno Jr 3s
225 Jofeph 100 228 243-
245 247 Johannah 89 John
113 206-210 220 243 249
John Jr 87 104 205 223
224 226 227 252 255
Jonath 247 Jonatha 87
Jonathan 98 206 223 224
226 228 244 Joseph 209
Martha 103 205 224 Mary
87 92 94 97 99 106 205
226 Mehetabel 114 245
Mehetabell 107 Mrs 83
Mofes 253 Moses 225
Nathan 223 247 Nathaniel
210 Rebecka 107 Rebekah
243 Richard 209 Sam 210
Samll 98 246 247 Samll Jr
99 223 Samuel 83 87 205-
207 209 228 243 245 249
Samuel Jr 92 105 224 226
Samuell 228 Sarah 87 98
114 208 223 228 255
Stephen 227 Thomas 226
DRESER, see DRESSER
DRESSER, Abigail 290 Amos
281 299-301 Ann 296
Benjamin 277 291 Bethiah
280 Daniel 273 273 280
282 283 285 293 Daniel Jr
291 David 280 281 300

205 William 205
FRAZER, Colen 83 Colin 85
220 Collen 213 Collin 219
Ebenezar 219 Gerfhom 220
Jane 92 Mark 277 Moses
279 Nathan 91 92 273-275
277 279 Simon 213 Solomon
275
FRAZIER, Collin 226 Lawson
226

GAGE, Apphia 94 284
Deborah 282 Elifabeth 114
Elisabeth 108 280
Elizabeth 300 301 Hannah
116 300 301 Jane 290 Lucy
116 Lucy-Gage 299 Mary
278 Mercy 110 Nathanael
112 286 290 Samuel 302
Sam-Nor 300 302 Samuel-
Northend 116 286 299
Sarah 93 Thomas 94 278
282 284 286 288 Thos 280
William 116 286 301
GALLOWAY, Anne 111
GEAGE, Elifabeth 222 248
Johanna 101 John 222 Mary
98 244 254 Mehetabel 246
Mercy 88 101 248 251
Mofes 226 Nathanll 253
Samuel 250 Sarah 106 224
243 245 Tho 248 Thomas 98
106 226 244 246 250
Thomas Jr 222 Thomas Sr
222 Thos Jr 224 William
88 101 243-246 248 251
253 254
GOODWIN, Hannah 251
GRANT, Goodw 82
GREEN, Daniel 297 Dolly
302 Lydia 115 Thomas 115
297 300 302
GREENOUGH, Daniel 227
Elifab 99 Epps 244 Hannah
100 John 245 Mary 220
Richard 244 Robert 100
245 Robert Jr 227 Robt
220 Robt Jr 228 244 Robt
Sr 88 Samuel 228 Sister
88
GUTTRIDG, Benj 216 Deborah

216 Ebenezer 216 John 216
Samuel 216 Sarah 216

HAFEN, Br 205 206 Edward
84 214 216 Hephzibah 205
Joan 84 John 216 Sarah
206
HAFLETINE, Abraham 82
Robert 206 Samuel 208
HAFSEN, Br 81
HAFUN, Edna 203 Edward 203
Hannah 203
HALE, Betty 288 Bradstreet
296 David 225 Dr 113
Dorothy 294 Edna 91 212
Goodm Jr 212 Jofeph 225
Joseph 301 Martha 113 290
Mary 291 293 Moses 292
Thomas 91 William 112 288
290 291 293 294 296 301
HAMMON, Bridget 89 102
David 103 250 254 255
Hannah 107 Jofeph 250
Mary 103 249 254
Nathanael 249 Nathanll
102 250 Nathll 247
Phinehas 255 Thomas 249
HAMMOND, David 278 292
David Jr 110 281-284 292
Ester 300 Hannah 210 247
Joanna 278 292 John 292
301 Jonathan 246 Mary 93
108 282 Nathanael 289
Nathll 246 Oliver 112 289
Phinehas 281 Sarah 111
113 290 292 Susanna 284
Tho 210 Tho Sr 247 Thomas
283 300 301
HAMON, see HAMMON
HAMOND, see HAMMOND
HARDY, Hannah 222 Samuel
209
HARRIC, Bridget 206 John
208 Nathaniel 206 208 210
Sarah 210
HARRICE, Bridgett 217
Dorcas 84 218 Edward 214
Elizabeth 83 207 218
Hannah 209 Jane 211 John
80 219 Joseph 213 Nath 83
Nathaniel 205 207 209 211

TODD, Abigail 96 299 Abner
223 Afa 97 115 Amoz 289
Anna 299 Anne 96 113 Asa
277 295 296 299 Benjamin
116 281 299-302
Brattlebank 249 Br 81 214
Caleb 301 Daniel 105 250
273 278 289 299 301
Daniel Jr 115 297 David
114 280 294 297 Dudley
296 Eben 279 Ebenezer 255
Edna 296 Ednah 95
Elifabeth 116 252
Elisabeth 294 296 299
Elizabeth 97 215 277
Elizebeth 300 George 116
287 302 Goodm Jr 212
Hannah 106 107 115 212
246 295 302 Henery-Bailey
303 Hester 224 James 91
96 98 112 113 205 222 224
226 243 244 246 274 289
292 293 296 299 Jane 115
254 299 Jedidiah 298
Jenny 296 Jeremiah 93 105
243 279 280 282 285-287
Jno 102 247 Joanna 285
297 Jofeph 92 226 Jofhua
253 John 84 96 110 203
214 215 217 220 222 223
226 247 250 252 253 277
278 280 281 298 299 John
Jr 91 111 214 249 251 254
255 276 280 296 John Sr
254 John 3d 115 Jonathan
105 107 226 274-277 279
282 286 296 Joseph 287
298 Joshua 292 Lucy 116
Lydia 102 Mary 91 98 110
220 222 251 282 292 297
Mehetabel 244 292
Mehetable 106 Mrs 84 102
112 Moses 291 293 298
Nathan 116 279 301 302
Nathaniel 295 302 Nelfon
115 Nelson 298 303 Paul
289 Prifcilla 243 Ruth 91
108 249 Samll 219 280
Samuel 205 217 223 224
243 249 Sarah 91 114 276
289 294 Soloman 298

Sufanna 224 Sufannah 90
103 Susanna 288 Thomas
112 203 222 223 254 288
289 291-293 295 296 298
Wallingford 301 William
112 273 286 287 289-292
294-296 298
TREDWAL, Jonathan 284 Mary
284
TREDWELL, Jonathan 95 Ruth
95
TREDWELS, Jonathan 280
Ruth 280
TRUMBL, Br 81 Deborah 205
Hannah 206 John 205 206
Joseph 206 Mary 206
TRUMBLE, Br 211 Deborah
203 211 Elifabeth 98
Goodwife 82 Hannah 227
John 80 203 205 208
Joseph 205 207 Judah 88
98 208 223 227 Mary 90
103 207 223
TUCKER, James 78
TULLAR, David 77
TUTTLE, Lucy 106

WAINWRIGHT, Sarah 211
Simon 211
WALKER, Hannah 222
Patience 224 Rebeka 226
Richard 222 224 226 227
Tabitha 224
WALLEY, Mr 284
WALLINGFOR, Margaret 227
Nicholas 227
WALLINGFORD, Nicholas 99
210 226 Sarah 226
WARRIN, Henry 295
WATFON, Hannah 204 John 82
204
WATSON, John 205
WEFT, John 221 Nathaniel
204 Twiford 204
WEICOM, Abigail 207 Daniel
204 206 207 209 223
Daniel Jr 216 218 Danll
222 225 Danll Jr 220
Elifabeth 225 Francis 207
Hannah 222 Hephzibah 223
John 207-209 211 214 216